## Praise for *The Full Body Yes*

"In *The Full Body Yes*, Scott Shute shares a fascinating tale, well-told, making a heartfelt case for self-awareness, full presence, and compassion. I couldn't stop reading."

**DANIEL GOLEMAN,** PhD, author of the *New York Times* bestseller *Emotional Intelligence*

"Writing with vulnerability, humor, and compassion, Scott Shute shares his insights and life lessons in *The Full Body Yes*. You will see yourself in these pages and truly enjoy the journey to more connection with yourself and with the people you lead."

**SHARON SALZBERG,** author of *Lovingkindness* and *Real Change*

"Scott Shute is an admired leader within LinkedIn, where he has helped individuals and organizations transform. In *The Full Body Yes*, Scott gives you the secret sauce that will help you transform your work and life—from the inside out."

**RYAN ROSLANSKY,** CEO of LinkedIn

"Scott Shute is a shining beacon for us all. His writing is vulnerable and powerful. His journey is our journey. *The Full Body Yes* is a delicious, life-changing tale of learning how to fully love."

**OSHOKE ABALU,** co-founder of Love & Magic Company

"This book is such a gift. I couldn't put it down. Scott Shute offers us no more and no less than the stories of his own life, and his courage, vulnerability, and learnings along the way have so much to teach us."

**SCOTT KRIENS,** co-creator of 1440 Multiversity and chairman of Juniper Networks

"Scott Shute sits at the intersection of the modern workplace and ancient wisdom traditions. His simple wisdom on how to change the world by changing ourselves is true for all ages and could not come at a better time. This inspiring book helped me see that I am a lovely work in progress and so is the world."

**CHIP CONLEY,** founder of Joie de Vivre Hospitality and author of *Wisdom at Work*

"Through captivating personal stories, *The Full Body Yes* clearly demonstrates how important it is to reclaim your power by deeply knowing yourself. This shift in awareness can positively impact your life and work. Scott Shute has created a greatly needed road map to reinvigorate the inner space of the mind and heart. This medicine is especially valuable during challenging times. *The Full Body Yes* is for anyone who is looking to bring a deeper meaning into their life and work."

**YUNG PUEBLO,** author of *Inward*

"In *The Full Body Yes*, Scott Shute shows us that optimism, self-awareness, and compassion aren't just feel-good concepts—they're how we build a great career and a great life."

**MIKE ROBBINS,** author of *We're All in This Together*

"Scott Shute is a masterful storyteller. His stories bring us right into the heart of the human experience and our deepest desires to find meaning and connection. Writing with vulnerability, he shows us that the fulfillment we seek lies right in the midst of our business challenges and personal challenges. The transformation happens from the inside out, and *The Full Body Yes* inspires and uplifts us so we can engage wholeheartedly and humbly in that process."

**TAMI SIMON,** founder of Sounds True

# THE
# FULL
# BODY
# YES

# Change Your Work and Your World from the Inside Out

THE **FULL BODY YES**

# SCOTT SHUTE

HEAD OF MINDFULNESS AND
COMPASSION PROGRAMS AT LINKEDIN

●● **PAGE TWO** BOOKS

Cataloguing in publication information is
available from Library and Archives Canada.
ISBN 978-1-77458-001-1 (hardcover)
ISBN 978-1-77458-036-3 (ebook)

Page Two
pagetwo.com

Edited by Lisa Thomas-Tench and Amanda Lewis
Copyedited by Melissa Edwards
Proofread by Alison Strobel
Jacket design by Peter Cocking and Taysia Louie
Jacket and interior illustrations by Brian Tong
Interior design by Fiona Lee
Printed and bound in Canada by Friesens
Distributed in Canada by Raincoast Books
Distributed in the US and internationally
by Publishers Group West, a division of Ingram

21 22 23 24 25   5 4 3 2 1

scottshute.com
thefullbodyyes.com

*For my parents, Ed and Jeri,*

*who showed me how to live.*

# CONTENTS

# INTRODUCTION

**H**I FRIEND,

I'm so glad you're here.

We, and by that I mean all of us here in the working world, need your help in changing work from the inside out. We have an opportunity to shape the consciousness of our workplaces by introducing more compassion.

There's really nothing that unique about the workplace. It's just another group of humans, doing their thing, bumping up against each other. A place to learn the lessons of life. We could learn the same lessons on a farm, in a family, being a teacher, or living in a monastery. Somehow over the years we've gotten into this strange pattern of thinking about work as "bad" and the rest of our lives as "good."

The simple truth is that it starts with us. Organizations are just a collection of individuals. When we develop ourselves as individuals, the organization evolves too.

If we want work to be a more humane place, it starts with us.

If we want to be more fulfilled, happier, more joyful, it starts with us. If we want to change the world, it starts with us.

The challenge is that we're usually just focused on ourselves. Me. Me. Me. And when we're this focused on our own lives, our own agenda, our own story, it's hard to be aware of others. It's hard to serve others. We all end up with more of the same, which is less than we wanted.

You and I are probably similar in many ways.

Our careers (and lives) are sometimes a crapshoot—forward, backward, sideways, forward again. Following our nose like a bloodhound wandering in a forest on the scent of a rabbit: the rabbit of meaningful work.

We measure success compared to those around us. We're constantly seeking external validation for our own happiness. *What do others think of me? How will this be perceived? Am I enough?*

We're often chasing something we *think* will make us happy. More money. More prestige. More respect. More.

Maybe you're reading this book because you want to know how to climb the mountain, be successful, beat the system. Or maybe you have that gnawing, longing feeling inside that won't go away. The one saying that the hole of achievement can never be filled. The one that is hungry for more, but a different type of more. Something deeper. A more that leaves you full.

Whole.

Free.

Maybe both things are true.

This is not one of those boring books about work that you feel like you *should* read and then struggle your way through. This is a book about life, and how the lessons we learn apply to every aspect of our existence, including—and sometimes especially—our work.

This is a book about what I've learned, and sometimes about what I'm still struggling to learn. I'm going to tell you a lot of stories from my own life. I'll share with you my inner dialogue. For each of us, this is really where our development happens. It's usually not the actual events in life that we're learning from; it's in the shaping and changing and thrashing of the mind where our growth occurs. We're so focused on ourselves, the me, me, me, and I'm no different. So, sorry if it feels like it's about me. I mean for it to be about all of us, but the truth is, I *really* only *truly* know about me, and what's going on in my own head.

I'll share my failures. I've had some spectacular ones. I'm not ashamed; I've learned a lot from them. Besides, I know you have failed in similar ways. This does not make us failures. I've had some successes as well—just like you have—and I'm not ashamed of those either, because I've learned a lot from them too. But they don't make *us* successful any more than our failures make *us* failures.

So what does make us successful? *Ah.* That's what we're going to explore.

Okay, friend, I know you have many choices in how to spend your time, and I appreciate that we've gotten this far together. Here's my commitment to you. If you promise to stick with me, to see yourself in these stories, to see your own failures in my failures and your own successes in my successes, your own longing for something more in mine, then I promise you...

This will not suck.

SCOTT SHUTE
November 2020

P.S. If you're impatient and just want the summary, go ahead and skip all of my amazing life-changing stories and go right to page 207.

## PART I

# Know Yourself

Know the true definition
of yourself. That is essential.
Then, when you know your
own definition, flee from it.

**RUMI**

# 1

# KNOW YOUR OWN STORY

I CAN SEE THE red semi coming from a mile away. It's probably hauling wheat that's been stored over the winter. Now the price is better, and it's headed to the elevator to sell. I do the math in my head. A thousand bushels, sixty pounds per bushel. I'm not sure how much the truck weighs. Maybe another twenty thousand pounds. Eighty thousand pounds total. Forty tons. Speed limit is fifty-five. No one drives fifty-five around here.

I'm in a tiny 1980 Chevy Citation. Probably weighs three thousand pounds. I'm going seventy-five miles an hour. I'm fifteen, a freshman in high school. I'm driving home from track practice. Tears are streaming down my face. I have no idea why.

I wonder if I will feel any pain when I slip into the other lane.

I wonder what my funeral will be like. I imagine watching the whole thing from above. My parents are in shock. I've tried to tell them, but we are speaking different languages. I overhear snippets from the crowd.

"Just a freak accident."

"Maybe the sun got in his eyes."

"Maybe a deer. There are so many deer. Just last fall Raymond hit one. Rolled right over the top of his car—hardly touched the bumper but crushed in the roof. Wouldn't have believed it if I didn't see it."

My siblings are quiet, each one dealing in their own private way.

My girlfriend is beside herself. It happened a mile from her house. She'll have to drive past the spot every day on the way to school for the next two years. Possibly every day for the rest of her life.

I can see my English teacher crying. She's read my poetry. She has an uneasy feeling in her stomach but doesn't say anything. Doesn't want to add to my parents' pain.

The red semi is a half mile away.

I unbuckle my seatbelt and turn up the stereo as loud as it will go.

In my mind, I scan the crowd for my classmates. The funeral service is being held at the school because there are too many people to fit at the mortuary or the church. "He was so young. Such a shame. What a waste."

The girls are crying. Cal and Britt, the kids who have been bullying me, are in the back row, quietly laughing. Mike, my sort-of-best-friend, has red eyes.

I think, "The hell with all of you."

The semi is now a quarter mile away. I can see the trucker's cowboy hat in the fading light. I don't recognize him or the truck.

At the funeral the trucker is shaken. He apologizes to my parents. The truck's front end was mangled. As the rig went off the road, the trailer jackknifed and bent just a bit. They'll probably be able to use it again. The Chevy Citation disintegrated. Hard to imagine that it used to be a car. Once the truck finally stopped, the distraught trucker had hobbled back to help.

It was way too late.

"I don't know what happened," he said to the sheriff, who arrived an hour and fifteen minutes later. "I was right up on 'im. At the last moment he just come into my lane. Nothin' I could do." He stared at his hands, his face pale. "Nothin' I could do."

The semi is seventy yards away. I can see his face.

I stomp on the accelerator.

I'm ready. I clench my jaw.

"Don't!" I hear a voice inside, as close as my heartbeat.

I freeze, just long enough for the semi to whoosh past me. My car shimmies with the passing draft. Adrenaline has flooded my system, like I've just injected a gallon of coffee. I'm jumpy and shaking. I can feel blood thumping in my neck.

"Pull over."

I comply.

I turn down the next dirt road I come to and drive over the hill so no one will see me from the highway. I get out of the car and walk into an open field. The wheat is green and just past ankle high. I'm on my hands and knees, pounding the wheat-grass and dirt and screaming at the top of my lungs, sobbing. I hit the ground with my bare hand until the pain makes me angry, then I curse about that, screaming some more.

My body is racked with sobs. Blood from my hand is getting all over my sweatpants. I ignore it. I lay down in the wheat and feel the earth, cool and damp against my cheek.

Finally, spent from my raging, my body slows down.

"It's going to be okay. I'm here with you."

I soften. I listen.

"This will pass."

I breathe deeply. Inhale. Exhale. Inhale. Exhale.

"You are never alone."

I sit up in the young wheat, watching how it blows in waves. I hear meadowlarks, turtledoves, and quail. I see rabbits at the edge of the pasture in the field nearby. I smell a wild olive tree in full bloom. I am still shaking, my face hot and wet.

I breathe.

Inhale.

Exhale.

Inhale.

Exhale.

Inhale.

Exhale.

Spent. Nothing left to rage. I'm softening.

"Just trust. You're going to be fine."

I take in the infinite sky. Like me, the setting sun is softening, lighting up puffy cumulus clouds with fading pastel colors. Golden arcs of light pierce the clouds in places, radiating warmth.

I become aware of my breathing.

Inhale.

Exhale.

Inhale.

Exhale.

I can feel my heart beating. It's starting to slow down.

"I am always with you."

I don't need to say anything back.

## Actor or Engineer?

I grew up on a family wheat farm in Kansas in a place so rural that fast food was a two-hour round-trip drive away, but I survived adolescence. I was eighteen and the world stood at the ready in front of me.

It was decision time.

I had wanted to be an engineer since I was in second grade. Honestly, I wasn't even sure what that meant, but my oldest brother had done it. The way my parents talked about it made it glow for me. What I knew was that I was good at math, liked computers, and that engineers made a lot of money. Engineers understood how things worked from the inside out. They could probably take apart a remote control and put it back together again. Maybe I could design sweet gadgets like the ones James Bond used.

The movie *Wall Street* had come out. One of the primary characters was Gordon Gekko, whose motto was "Greed Is Good." According to my eighteen-year-old brain, getting an engineering degree and working for a big company was like selling my soul to the man. Yes, I wanted all the "stuff" that came with success. A nice house, vacations somewhere on a beach. Maybe even the social respect that came with it. I saw the look in people's eyes when they talked about engineers.

During my senior year I was the lead in our high school musical—*The Music Man*. I loved the rush of performing. I loved singing and the music that went with it. I especially loved the accolades. I was thinking about moving to New York and trying to make it on Broadway. This conversation was not particularly popular with my parents, especially my father. As a farmer born during the Great Depression, he knew the reality of making a living in this world. He didn't exactly say no, but he made it clear which path he'd rather support with his hard-earned money.

But the dream of an extraordinary life was burning white hot.

A few years earlier, I had discovered and awakened my sense of spirituality. I had found a path that was quite different from the little country church that we attended every Sunday. I was interested in meditation and inner contemplation, exploring the unseen worlds within. I was starting to understand that there was something more to life than dollars. Still, that voice was hard to hear sometimes.

The choice seemed black or white. Sell my soul, or follow my spiritual bliss and discover my True Self. I was torn. Confused. Frustrated. I could do anything. That didn't make it any easier to choose.

I was in contemplation one day, having a conversation with The Thing. Call it what you want—the Divine, God, the Universe, Source, your True Self. Humbled, I had essentially thrown up my hands and said, "I don't know! I need a little help here. What am I supposed to do?"

In that moment, in that conversation, I experienced what I call The Full Body Yes, where knowing happens at a deeper level than the mind could ever fathom. It happened in my entire being, and a deep sense of peace with the answer took over where chaos had ruled.

I was at peace. I smiled. Relaxed. Exhaled.

The clarity came with a message, an intuition: "Maybe you can change work from the inside out."

## The Fab Review

I'm bored. The kind of restless bored I remember from grade school. The kind where you're staring out at the trees and dreaming about recess.

I'd be staring out the window if there were one. Instead I'm doodling on my notebook. I'm drawing little geometric designs, writing my name in Japanese, trying to draw faces, experimenting with my signature, attempting to design a new font.

I'm twenty-eight. I'm starting to figure out this whole sales thing. I've been assigned to a very important account. It's kind of a big deal. Huge responsibility. And stress.

I'm in the middle of day two of a quality review. I've traveled with a group of quality managers from my customer's company in California to do a deep dive on our "fab" in Texas. The fab is a billion-dollar plant that builds semiconductors.

We've got many. In Texas. The Philippines. Japan. It's incredibly complicated, billions of little switches built into a little black chip the size of your fingernail. These chips go into the things that go into the things that go into the things that you might use, like a computer, a car, or internet service.

This particular customer is one of our largest and most important. They buy nearly a million dollars' worth of these little chips from us every day to build hard drives, so my team from headquarters is on high alert, laughing at the customers' jokes. For the HQ team, this is like Christmas. The leader even wore a tie, though not one that's been in fashion at any point during the previous twenty years. Normally, a quality manager doesn't get much love, squirreled away deep in the recesses of the organization, lost behind the engineering leaders and the sales guys. In this case, the customer has come to see them specifically, and to talk about their baby for two days straight. For me, though, it's a slow form of torture. Ugh.

I enjoy the relationship-building part of my job. This part, however, trapped deep in the bowels of "the factory," is killing me. I mostly know what's going on but have zero interest. Occasionally my customer will ask a detailed question about process and we'll dive into a forty-five-minute discussion that might as well be in Swahili. For these parts of the conversation, I add no value. I've connected this little family of semiconductor process-quality geniuses together, and now I'm like a parent on the sideline of a school dance, unneeded, restless, awkward. Staring at my hands. Wondering when it's all going to end. Except I'm in charge of the agenda, so I know exactly when it's going to end. Forever from now.

I go back to my doodles. I think about learning to write in Klingon.

This doesn't feel like changing the world to me. There's *got to* be something more. This is soul crushing. I *cannot* do this forever. I've got to get out of here. This meeting. This job.

I wonder what my life would have been like if I were on Broadway. I look out an imaginary window and sigh.

When is it going to be fun?

## The Start-Up

Over a decade later, in 2009, I'm waiting for my small team at the back of an Italian restaurant in the middle of the day. We've been meeting here nearly every week for the past two years. Today will be the last time. Three years ago, I had self-funded a start-up, placing a bet on myself with a good chunk of our family's life's savings. There was a small team counting on me. Ajay. Karen. Jason. We were trying to make big things happen. Today it is all going to be over. I am shutting it down.

In 2006, I had decided to create my own company on top of my day job, and fill it with all the things I liked. My great-grandfather had moved west to Kansas to find adventure in the open spaces of the prairie, to find his truth. One hundred and twenty years later, I had moved west to California to find my own adventure. My truth. Now here I was, creating a Silicon Valley start-up. The American Dream. I figured it was my path to freedom. If my start-up was successful, I could quit my day job. I wanted to be free from Corporate America. Free from jerk bosses. Free from politics.

And then what? Well, then I'd be free to set my own schedule and do what I wanted. I could spend more time with my kids. I could be there for all of my family's important moments. Freedom.

In the beginning it was fantastic. I was learning something new every day, about every aspect of running a business, building a company. After three years, though, the bloom was fading. Now, I am spending twenty hours a week on my start-up, in addition to my fifty-hour-per-week day job. I began doing the start-up life to get freedom and spend time with my kids. But I am finding myself sneaking away from my kids at night and on the weekends to be with my start-up project, a mistress with an insatiable appetite. Every day, I love it less and less. And, I wonder, what if it does take off? What if it becomes a raging success? Then there would be board meetings, shareholder expectations, a company to run. I wouldn't be able to step aside and let someone else take over. My commitment would grow larger every year.

I would be shackled to the mast of my own miserable boat to freedom.

The weekend before this Italian restaurant meeting, I had gone to a seminar with my spiritual community, a yearly gathering I deeply look forward to. It was a chance to reflect, to stop and connect with something deeper. My work dilemma pressed on me, gripping my chest with anxiety. I tried to let go, to check in with something bigger. I knew what my ego wanted. That wasn't helping. My friend Ben had asked me a question that I had pondered all weekend: "What does your True Self want?"

I knew I needed to follow my heart. I went within and tried to listen. Tried to quiet the noise. To tamp down the distractions that chipped away at my foundation. To tame my ego.

In contemplation, I knew the path forward.

Another Full Body Yes.

It was time to let the start-up go.

I relaxed. Softened. Felt lighter.

But I was worried about the others on the team. They were counting on me. For Ajay, the start-up was his primary source of income. He'd have to go find a job. Jason was in between jobs and helping out. Karen was acting as a consultant. I was paying her to keep the ship afloat. She had other clients.

So I sit in the restaurant, waiting, nervous about what I am going to say. I don't want to let anyone down, but I also know that it is time. I stiffen my resolve. Staring at my chai latte, I wonder why I gave up drinking.

Ajay walks in alone, wearing a peculiar look. After some chit chat, he comes right out with it.

"Hey, man," he begins. "The guys and I got together over the weekend. We talked it over. I was voted as the one who should talk with you." I furrow my brow, waiting.

"I'm sorry, my friend."

I wait some more, nodding for him to continue. He swallows hard and then blurts it out.

"It's time to shut this thing down."

## Know Yourself

Each of us has a unique story to tell. Who we are. Where we came from. No one else in the world has that story. Only you can tell it.

At the same time, if we remove the detail, the context, our stories are similar to everyone else's.

We experience heartache. We have successes. We let ourselves and others down. We inspire others and make them laugh. We have plans that work out. We have plans that don't. We win. We lose. We sometimes succeed when we don't deserve to. We sometimes fail when it's not our fault. We can feel left out, disconnected. Or loved, understood, and gotten.

Life never gives us more than we can handle, but sometimes it's more than we can handle using the tools and habits we've adopted. Challenge creates growth if we're willing to listen, willing to have humility and be open to change.

These challenges play out at work, just like they play out at home. These lessons find us, whether we're a singer in a

Broadway musical or a salesperson at a semiconductor company. It doesn't matter if we work in a monastery or an office
building, the lessons will find us.

We are individual sparks of energy that are part of a universe of energy. At once unique, separate, yet fully connected.

When we know ourselves, we can see our own story clearly,
as if viewed from the outside. We can better understand the
choices we've made, and the choices we're likely to make again.

We can't change our story to this point; we can only recognize who we are.

And then the future, like a beautiful island emerging from
the mist on the horizon, is ours to write.

Why are you so enchanted
with this world,
When a mine of gold lies
within you?

**RUMI**

# 2

# THE SYSTEM

I STARE DOWN AT the Fast Passes in my hand, smirking. I have cracked the code. One real Fast Pass on top. Three fake ones underneath. We are headed to the front of the line at Disneyland.

I'm running through the plan in my mind, smiling inwardly at my cleverness.

Disneyland is not exactly my happy place. I do love the rides. The lines, not so much. I grew up on a farm, an hour from the nearest movie theater. We never stood in line, never really had to wait for anything.

I'm naturally impatient. In the family photo album, there are many (many!) pictures of me and my younger cousin as grade-schoolers "guarding" the cake. Birthdays, weddings, church socials, whatever. There we are with our devilish little grins, barely able to contain ourselves. Or maybe it was just me with the patience problem and my cousin was guilty by association. Either way, restricted by warnings from the ladies in charge about digging in, we were always ready, standing as close to the cake as possible so that the instant it was cut, we would be first in line.

I'm the youngest of five. My siblings are quite a bit older than me. We grew up playing a lot of cards and board games at our house. I was born with a competitive streak. I always wanted—no, *had to*—win. It drove my sisters crazy. I was always looking for an edge, a loophole, a way to bend the rules in my favor. In some ways, it's still true: in traffic, I move from lane to lane, trying to find the fastest one, even though I've read the research that says traffic would move more quickly if we all stayed in our lane.

At Disneyland, with my wife and teenage kids, I am looking for that same loophole. We had purchased the online guide, which is supposed to help us maximize our fun by predicting where the shortest lines are throughout the day and advising us on how to string the best experiences together most efficiently. I've spent twenty years as an operations leader. I like efficiency. I hate waste.

Let me explain that Fast Pass. It is a beautiful thing. It essentially allows you to go to a special part of the line where the wait is only five minutes instead of an hour or more. The problem is, you can only have one at a time. There are self-service machines that dispense Fast Passes. So, you're standing in front of Space Mountain at 10 a.m. and enter your park pass into the machine. You get back one Fast Pass, with an appointment time of, say, 11:30 a.m. You still have to wait until 11:30, but once that happens, you get to go to the front. If you try to get another pass before 11:30, the machine will spit out a little note that basically says, "Sorry, you can only have one Fast Pass at a time. Please come back later."

I saw the system.

I am wired to beat the system.

Once I find a loophole, the desire to beat the system burns like money from Grandma in a nine-year-old's pocket.

Beating the system means I am a winner. Beating the system means I am smarter and better than everyone else.

If I'm smarter and better, people will notice me. If they notice me, I will be liked. If I am liked, I will be safe.

I will be loved.

Beating the system has been my life strategy.

I noticed that the little "Sorry, you can only have one Fast Pass" notes that were coming out of the machine were exactly the same size and color as the Fast Pass tickets. I also noticed that each time we approached the ticket taker in the Fast Pass line, I would hand them a little stack of four tickets for the four of us. They never bothered to look at each one. They simply received the stack of tickets from me and placed them in their collected tickets pile.

I realized I could take each of our four actual Fast Passes and pair them with three of the "Sorry" notes, hand the ticket taker a little stack, and scoot our way to the front of the line. No one would ever know. We'd quadruple our fun. The blueprints for Operation Fake Fast Pass were complete.

Approaching the line, I smirk again, a loud smirk of deep knowing.

I am an expert at beating the system.

But another feeling rises up in my stomach. A sense of discomfort. Dis-ease. Winning isn't feeling as good as it used to.

For a while now, I've been starting to realize that the way I've been playing is not really winning. This emphasis on me, me, me is feeling more and more empty.

I've been trying to drop my immature habits. I've been growing and developing spiritually. I'm trying to be more aware of my impact on others. I had recently been having a sincere conversation with the Divine about how I might better serve all of life. How I might be more compassionate.

I mull over Operation Fake Fast Pass, lost in my thoughts, sorting out my strategy.

Then I hear it. The Voice.

"Seriously?" it says.

A long, pregnant pause. It has my attention.

"Is this what serving looks like to you?" it asks.

I look around at all the people waiting in line. They are just as deserving as I am. We are all equals. My little ticket charade is the same as passing each crowded line, packed with other families, waiting just the same as we are and saying (three times!), "I'm more important than you. Let me through."

I smile again at myself, but this time with a different meaning. Chastised, I throw the "Sorry" notes in the trash and get back in line.

## Feedback

"I need more from you."

It's many years before Disneyland, and I already think I am winning. But still, working in sales at twenty-six, I find myself sitting in my manager's office. Adam—that manager—is just a couple of years older than me. We are all finding our way.

"What does that mean?" I ask. I am genuinely confused. I thought things were going well. Something doesn't feel right. I don't even know where to start.

"I don't know. I can't put my finger on it. It's an important time in the account. I just need more from you." He stares at me with kind eyes. He's a good guy. He's trying. He's probably getting pressure from his manager.

I think hard, and my inner monologue goes something like this: "I guess there's always more I could give. Even if I'm already doing 'A' work, there's always room to get to A+." When we are done with our talk, I go back to my desk and stare at my email. I stare at my account plan. I think about each of my customer relationships.

I have no clue what "more" looks like.

Over the next few months, I search for ways to give more, to do more. I stay in the office a bit longer each night. In the absence of a real idea, the only thing I can think of is to work harder or, at least, longer. I am desperately in search of the A+, but it is elusive. I am just hanging on, trying to figure out who I am and where I fit in. Trying to do the best I can, while not losing myself in the process.

Adam doesn't bring it up again. I don't get any specific advice or requests. I'm left with vague dissatisfaction.

*More.*

The itch that can never be scratched away. The one that leaves me feeling aimless, a treadmill to nowhere.

Six months later there are some account shake-ups, reorganization. Apparently someone, somewhere higher up, has decided they need "more" from the leadership team as well, and suddenly I have a new manager. Mahmoud. He's quirky. Smart. Weathered. Smokes. Curses like a pirate. He is a free-range chicken. He's older. We think he's *ancient*, older than we can imagine. He's thirty-six.

On the morning of the reorg announcement, Mahmoud calls our little team of three together. His pep talk is short.

"I'm not sure what you guys have been doing. I think we have a big opportunity here. We're gonna kick some ass." He makes brief eye contact with each of us. "Any questions?"

We steal quick glances at each other. We're a little dazed. Quiet. This might be the shortest meeting in the history of meetings.

An hour later Mahmoud swings by my desk. It's time for our first one-on-one meeting.

"Let's go for a walk," he says. It's another beautiful, sunny day in San Jose. We head down to the parking lot so Mahmoud can have a smoke. I try to position myself upwind.

We make small talk for a bit. A very short bit. Mahmoud doesn't mess around. He's a sales guy, so he knows how to build relationships. He also seems to have calculated the minimum amount of time required to do so. He gets right to it.

"How do you think things are going?" He cocks his head. Looks directly at me.

"Umm. I don't know. Seems like things are going okay." I really don't know what he's looking for.

"And how are you doing?"

"I'm fine, I guess." I'm guarded. I'm definitely not ready to share my feelings with Mahmoud.

"No, I mean, how are you performing?" He takes a drag on his cigarette, looks at me with a smile that says he's finally getting to talk about what he wants to talk about.

I'm really confused. Alarmed. This doesn't sound good.

"I think okay. I don't know. What do you mean?" I can feel the anxiety rising in my throat. I don't know where this is coming from.

Mahmoud tells me that things are not going well for the account. That things are not going well for me.

"They wanted to put you on a plan, but I told them to hold off. I think I can help you." Mahmoud says this matter-of-factly, like he's reading the weather report.

"A plan?" I've moved way past alarmed. The color slips from my face. My eyebrows rise halfway to my hairline.

I'm seriously, genuinely confused.

"A performance plan." Now Mahmoud looks confused. "Didn't Adam ever talk to you?" He scrunches one side of his face, looking frustrated, but not with me.

"Not really. I thought things were going okay."

"Um, no." In his own way, Mahmoud is trying to console me. His form of kindness involves being blunt.

"Look, Adam told me he needed more from me. I thought I was doing 'A' work and that, sure, I could always give more. I could be an A+." I'm incredulous. My voice is getting louder. "Instead, apparently, I was a D, about to be put on a plan. About to be fired? Come on! What the hell?"

This is all happening very fast. My body is still catching up. My shoulders slump. I look down at my shoes. How did I miss this? How have I been so far removed from reality? What other stories have I been telling myself that are just wrong? My truth is coming undone, crumbling. I feel the instability. "He never frickin' told me."

Mahmoud sighs. Shakes his head. Smiles in a way that says, "I'm sorry."

"Well, at least never in a way that I could hear," I say. I stare off at nothing. Dumbstruck.

I feel nauseous.

Mahmoud puts out his cigarette. He softens slightly. "It's gonna be okay. I'll work with you. I think you can do it. We're gonna kick some ass."

I let out a long exhale and nod, lips tight.

Determined.

## Going for More and Ending Up with Less

That conversation with Mahmoud was a turning point. He helped me figure some things out. He helped me understand how to communicate with the leadership team. Things started clicking. I got it. After starting my career in sales, I found my way into people management in customer operations at another company. It was a great fit. I rocketed my way up the ladder, promoted four times in five years.

About a decade after that conversation with Mahmoud, I was a senior director, leading a team of hundreds. My manager, a VP—who was my mentor, sponsor, and friend—had just left the company under cloudy circumstances. I was his top lieutenant, so I was the new leader on an interim basis. But the environment wasn't great. For ten years we had been the company and the group that could do no wrong, but the whole business was changing, becoming tougher. The leadership team was changing and hardening as well. Now there was a dark cloud around everything we did.

It was painful, but I was *so close* to the top of the mountain. After nine months, the senior VP I was reporting to informed me that the role I'd been playing on a temporary basis would officially be mine.

Here. It. Was.

The top of the mountain.

I was going to be a VP before I turned thirty-five.

And I had never been so miserable at work in my entire life.

And as soon as I could see the top of the mountain, it fell away. The promotion never happened. I was *shocked* when my manager reorganized and put a few of his operations functions together. I was hurt that I wasn't asked to lead the new combined function. I was raw. I felt like I had given so much. I had moved five times in six years, three of them internationally, with two little kids. I had traveled way too much, sacrificed too much, and nearly ruined my marriage. I had been instrumental to the growth and success of the group, had hired nearly every leader in the entire organization. It was my baby.

It was my identity.

Then, my job was eliminated and I was left absolutely devastated.

Then, over the next few years, my role was eliminated twice more.

Each time I found a new role on the inside. Each time was stressful. Each time life was trying to show me a better way, but I was holding on to an old dream with both hands, refusing to listen.

Each time life was trying
to show me a better way,
but I was holding on to an
old dream with both hands,
refusing to listen.

## The Magic Is The Full Body Yes

Back at Disneyland, I start thinking about how I could make it more fun for my kids while we wait.

I chat up our line neighbors, trying to get them to laugh or smile.

I try to enjoy just living in the moment.

I am starting to be more deeply aware of a different system at play. Turns out that the path to happiness is to live a life of compassion, to be of service to the world, instead of just my own needs. To truly be aware of others I first need to be aware of myself. To love others and their true nature, I first need to love myself and recognize my own true nature. To be responsible and take action for others, I first need to be responsible and take action for myself.

Here, at Disneyland, I identify the system. The most important system.

I wonder if I will ever crack the code.

I wonder if I will ever understand.

I wonder if I will ever win.

Like learning a new board game, once we know the rules, we can play more skillfully. We can have more fun. We develop an appreciation and understanding of our own story. We learn why we're making the choices we're making. We become aware of our own patterns. This awareness gives us choice.

We can learn to navigate the external systems in our lives. To hack our internal systems, slipping past our own defenses. To see the prison that our amygdala and our negative minds have created to keep us safe.

We can choose to stay, or we can choose to step out of the cage and fly.

And we can listen to a deeper voice—that internal voice that knows. The one that is infinite. The one that is whole and has no outside needs. We can redefine success, for both ourselves and for others.

The chains fall away and we are free to move. We feel a deep sense of satisfaction, a deep sense of contentment, like a glorious exhale. We feel alignment between our nervous systems and our mind. We feel it in our entire being. The Full Body Yes.

We can establish a new destination for our lives, a new measure of success. A new measure for winning.

We can change the game.

It's not just about safety and survival.

It's about freedom.

When you lose all sense of self

The bonds of a thousand

chains will vanish.

**RUMI**

# 3

# THE TRAP IS SET

"**S**HUTE—DID YOU THROW up yet?"

I'm a freshman in high school. It's fifteen minutes before the game starts. My JV basketball coach knows the drill. I've been doing this since sixth grade. Every game, every music performance, every first date.

I seem calm on the outside, but inside my stomach is like a basket of hummingbirds. Most of the time it's not a big deal. Every once in a while, it surprises and embarrasses me.

I drive up to the house of the most popular girl at school. We're headed to the movies. It's a long drive to the nearest theater. Considering it's a first date, we'll be spending a lot of time together.

I knock on the front door and she appears. Tall and blond in a way that reminds me I have no idea what I'm doing. We're both nervous. I immediately ask if I can use her restroom. She's kind and points the way.

My nerves have gotten the best of me and now I'm sick. I stay in the restroom for five full minutes before going back out to greet my date. Not the smooth start I was hoping for.

I'm wound too tight.

As the youngest of five much older siblings, I grew up faster, had different expectations. I always felt more comfortable around older kids and adults than I did with kids my own age. It was what I knew. I also grew up in super-rural Kansas. In elementary school, I had seven kids in my class. Our family lived farthest from town, so we were the first ones on the bus and the last ones off, an hour each way.

I read a lot.

There were no "play dates." My classmates lived too far away, and my parents were too busy. I grew up by myself, with my older siblings and my nearby cousin. I enjoyed it, exploring a few thousand acres with my black lab, or tearing around on a dirt bike. As a kid, I didn't think about it too much. I was just living life, roaming. I loved living on the farm.

That all changed when I was old enough to work. Suddenly there were bigger expectations and responsibilities. By the time I was fourteen, I was driving (legally), taking care of fifteen hundred hogs, and graduating to more serious field work with a tractor.

The surrounding landscape was quiet, idyllic. My inner landscape was chaos. The raging hormones, the body changes, the anxiety.

My dad was a busy man. He was managing a complicated farming operation. He and mom were also raising five kids, each with their own activities, sporting events, and needs. He was a solid man, a pillar of the church, respected in the community.

And . . . I wanted more from him. I wanted him to play catch with me. I wanted to go fishing with him after church on Sunday. I wanted a hug and an "I love you." I wanted him to notice me.

I was born with a competitive streak. Cards. Board games. Running to the mailbox and back. Everything was a contest to be won. When sister #2 left for college, I started seventh grade, transitioning into being an only child, alone in the big farmhouse with my parents and the memories of my siblings. It was my time.

I narrowed my young eyes and decided that I would be the best.

At everything.

Each of them had their thing. My oldest brother was the academic, an engineer, and already a successful businessman. Brother #2 was a great musician. He had toured America in a rock band before coming back to run the farm with my dad. My oldest sister was also a gifted musician, an accomplished pianist. Sister #2 was fantastic at sports.

I would play each of their games. And win. Not just win. Dominate. I wanted to win in a way that all other past winners were forgotten. I wanted to win in a way that all previous trophies and memories and banners of victory were replaced by mine.

And then, maybe then...

My father might just notice me. Might just give me a hug.

It was a powerfully effective motivation strategy.

Being a student at a very small school, there was opportunity. I was the quarterback in football, the point guard in basketball, ran hurdles in track, and was a shortstop and starting pitcher in baseball. My little league team won state two years in a row. I was in marching band, got a "1" at state for singing, and was the lead in my high school musical. I won state speech contests, state math contests, got straight As, and got a perfect score on the math portion of the ACT.

And I was undeniably, tragically miserable. Desperately digging a hole of achievement that would never be deep enough to bury my pain.

In the summer before my sophomore year, during my annual physical exam for school sports, I asked my doctor about why I was throwing up. He explained how my brain was sending far more signals than my body could absorb. My mind was trying to do way more than my body could handle.

The doctor essentially told me I needed to chill out or I wouldn't live long as an adult. I took it in, considered his advice, nodding, not mentioning that I was pretty sure I wasn't going to make it to adulthood.

## Simon

"Okay guys, let's take grounders—lines at short and second, throws to first and third."

Coaching my son's little league team is bringing back everything I loved about baseball as a kid. Now I get to be ten years old again. We're trying to find that balance between having a great time and getting better, building a winning team. When I was a kid, I played baseball only in the summer. Fall was for football. Basketball in winter. Track in the spring. My high school for the first two years had sixty kids. Total. I switched schools for my junior and senior years to a bigger nearby town and then had just over a hundred.

I got to play everything.

Now we know how to build champions—we specialize. Olympic champions start gymnastics at age two. Tiger Woods started playing golf at two. They are lauded as heroes. My son is eleven. He's made the local all-star team. He started playing when he was nine. Probably too late. He wants to keep getting better. He'd like to play in high school. We've signed him up for travel ball. This involves my wife driving him to practice in rush hour traffic three times a week and to all-day tournaments for the whole family two hours away on the weekend, all year long. My daughter plays competitive soccer. Same deal. Practice all the time. Games and tournaments on the weekend. Always training. She's seven.

We're not blind. We see how ridiculous it is. But how do you say no? Your child wants to get better at something, is passionate. You want to give them every opportunity to achieve. To be happy.

A kid named Simon is on the recreational little league team that I'm coaching. He's always late, and often doesn't even show. Simon has that faraway look in his eyes, like he's out of his body. He plays a lot of right field. Ten-year-olds rarely hit a ball to right field. If they did hit a ball to right field against our team, they would have a home run. He's there, but he's not there. During games I've seen him wandering around the outfield looking for bugs, his glove forgotten on the ground twenty steps behind him. I find myself doing a lot of yelling at Simon.

"Simon! Are you with us?"

"Simon! Pay attention!"

"Simon! It's your turn to bat. Get out there!"

"Simon... where'd you go, buddy?"

We're in the middle of practice. Most of the boys are eager to go, let loose from the shackles of school. They are here to compete. To get better with each at bat. To get better with each grounder that they field. To quietly, silently test themselves against yesterday. Against an opponent still to come. Against each other.

"Hey Simon, we're doing grounders. Get in one of those lines at second or short." He's sitting in the dugout, taking an extraordinarily long time to find some gum from his backpack.

The other boys have sprinted to their places and are eagerly engaged, whooping and chattering. Simon saunters over to me. I'm in the middle of the drill, hitting ground balls one after the other, each one placed with precision and effortlessness, crafted from years of practice, of diligence, of eagerness.

"Coach Scott?"

"Yes, Simon," I exhale, slowing down a bit to take him in, frustrated.

"What are we doing again?"

I'm incredulous. I look at him like he's an alien. My heart is suddenly pounding, and I can feel adrenaline in my veins. I want to shake him.

"What?! Look! We're taking grounders! Two lines!"

"Coach?" He looks sincere. Or, maybe he's dazed from his ADHD meds. I can never tell.

I try to slow down to hear him. I'm still frustrated, but I slow down.

"What, Simon?"

"When are we going to have fun?"

## Finding My Way

"Where did you go?"

I am thirteen, and my older brother has returned to the farm after having left for the long weekend. He had gone to Houston, a twelve-hour drive. Six months before, he had gone to St. Louis, an eight-hour drive. There had been a vague explanation about some sort of music festival.

A year or so earlier he had moved back home to work on the farm with my dad. Before that he had been touring with a band along the east coast, trying to make a living as a rock star. As the stages and paychecks got smaller and smaller, he got weary of the road. Farming seemed better and better. He even met a girl and got engaged. She came to visit from Upstate New York, wondering if there would be buffalo and Native Americans roaming around. She saw what life was really like. The beautiful open skies. The friendly neighbors. The hard work. The isolation.

She didn't come back.

My brother was settling into farm life, but his travels had changed him. These long weekends away held the clue to what those changes were.

He was being cagey about the whole thing.

A few days after his trip to Houston, my sisters and I are at his house, the original farmhouse where my dad grew up, on the original homestead that our great-grandfather had established in the 1880s. George Emerson Shute had traveled here by wagon from New Hampshire, searching for the truth of his new life. He had left the comfort of family and routine and city life and explored into the wilderness with nothing but the constant wind, the long grass, and a dream of something more. He ventured into the void and came home. He found his truth.

Secrets are hard to come by in this community. If you go to Houston for the weekend, everyone knows. They may or may not care. But they'll know.

Every Tuesday night, Nettie Seems will call the house at seven o'clock. Nettie is ninety-two years old. Whoever forgets what time it is and answers the phone will get to talk with her. Everyone else scatters, suddenly gets very busy. She collects news for the *Jewell County Record*—the local paper. She is calling to ask what news we have.

"News" is all relative. There's a section in the paper called the "Highland Township Update." This is the thirty-six-square-mile township that we live in, one of many in the county. It's mostly made up of the thirty folks who go to our little country church. Many are the same families that came from the original homesteaders in the 1880s. These roots, these patterns, run deep.

A typical news flash in the Highland Township Update might read something like:

Ed and Jeri Shute were pleased to host their nephew Philip, along with wife Kaitlin, for the weekend, visiting from Broken Bow, NE. Their son Cole has a birthday coming up. Jeri made a cherry pie for the occasion. She says the chokecherries are nearly in season and soon there will be jam.

No one has told Nettie that my brother went to Houston.

No one tells me why my brother went to Houston.

I am thirteen. My sisters and I want to know. We are going to camp out in his living room until he tells us.

He doesn't want to, which makes the secret even more delicious, a bit dangerous. We aren't leaving without an answer. Finally, he relents. During his travels he had come across a different spiritual path. During these long weekends he attends a type of seminar or retreat.

I understand the magnitude of the secrecy. We live in a small place. The type of place where "different" is an insult. Different is scary. Different is dangerous.

This is big. No wonder he has been being cagey. No wonder no one is talking about it.

"They" would shun him.

"They" would gossip about him.

"They" would say he's going to burn in everlasting hell.

I'VE ALWAYS had a deep connection with the Divine. I could sense it in the way the light streams through the clouds. I could sense it in the frogs that sang their lusty songs in the summertime. When I was quiet, still, I could feel it, pulsing within. It was the calm to my rage. Sometimes I could even feel it in church.

We attended one of those tiny country Methodist churches from a Norman Rockwell painting. I missed church only a handful of times in eighteen years: if I was sick with the flu or the road was closed due to snow. We were regulars, reliable as the sunrise. My extended family made up nearly half of the attendees. My dad and uncle led Sunday school after the main service. My mom led the children's choir. My grandma was the pianist until she was in her nineties. We all sang, played music, and acted in the Christmas or Easter play. I sang my first solo when I was five. I learned a lot in that little church. It shaped me.

But something else was awakening.

I could feel it.

Mostly church didn't make sense to me. To keep myself entertained, I counted the ceiling tiles (three hundred, exactly). I looked out the window and thought about fishing later with my uncle and cousin. I daydreamed. A lot.

At about age eleven, I started asking my parents questions that I didn't like the answers to. I loved God, but the way we were talking about It didn't match what I believed. What I believed was something else, something I had never seen written down, but I *knew*. I stopped asking my parents questions.

It's a lonely feeling to start building a secret.

Now, when my brother starts sharing about this other spiritual path he has found, he describes all the things I know to be true. All the things I already believe. Here they are, named. Written down.

I start weeping.

Tears are streaming down my face, my eyes large with awe. I have found what I have been searching for. Not for two or three years since turning eleven. For lifetime after lifetime after lifetime. Now, I have found my truth.

*My* truth. It doesn't need to be anyone else's.

I am home.

First,

The fish needs to say,

"Something ain't right with this

Camel ride—

And I'm feeling

So damn

Thirsty."

**HAFIZ**

# 4

# UNWRITTEN RULES

"ANITYA, WHAT DO you want to do?"

She exhales loudly, slowly shaking her head back and forth, dropping her eyes to her lap. She shrugs, deflated. Mutters, "Does it even matter?"

I have been mentoring Anitya off and on for six months. I'm leading global customer operations at LinkedIn. She has been working as a product manager on an adjacent team for the past couple of years. She is great at her job, a rising star. She is making progress, getting traction with a product that has been struggling. Her leadership team is taking notice. Her peers have good things to say about her. She has the world on a string.

She is miserable.

Anitya's journey had started early. In third grade, her mother, a successful software engineer, had bullied her school into bumping her up a grade. She knew all the math. She was bored. In middle school, she went to Kumon even though she had straight As. At thirteen, she studied, memorized, and drilled for hours with her sister to win the state spelling bee. She felt humiliated when she just missed the top five at nationals. She missed the word theileriasis (definition: "any of a group of livestock diseases caused by protozoan parasites of the genus *Theileria* [*Gonderia*], transmitted by tick bites," says the *Encyclopedia Britannica*[1]). She was mortified. Irritated that she didn't know what it meant. The memory of the judge informing her of her error still haunts her. Worse was her father's thin smile and faint praise: "*Almost* top five."

In high school she took as many STEM and AP classes as she could. She played field hockey and soccer, but she wasn't the captain. She was the student body vice president. She tied with fifteen other students with perfect grades for valedictorian. She got a 1540 out of 1600 on her SAT. She took it five times. Her father kept dropping in conversation that one of her cousins, Prakash, had gotten a 1570.

She did well at Carnegie Mellon, studying computer science in her mother's footsteps. She avoided the big parties. Didn't join a sorority. Didn't date, even though she got a lot of attention in her classes. She didn't love her classes. She got the first B of her life in the first semester as she adjusted to life away from home. It didn't happen again.

And here she was with one of the most coveted jobs at one of the most prestigious companies in the world, tearing it up, a raging success.

Miserable.

"I got accepted into Harvard," she tells me flatly. I had written her a letter of recommendation for business school a few months before.

"Seriously! Woah! That's amazing!" I say. She is half-smiling. It isn't hard to see her suffering. "And?"

"I dunno. I got rejected by Stanford."

"Okay, well, they clearly don't know what they're missing."

She gives me a wry smile.

"Anyway," I continue, "wasn't Harvard your first choice? Isn't that what you wanted?" Her eyes well up just a little. She quickly tries to hide it, sniffing quickly and hardening her posture. She bites her lower lip.

"Does that even matter?" she asks.

"What's going on?"

She is quiet for a very long time. Finally, she relents. It's time for it all to spill out.

"My life is a mess. I don't even know if I want to do this. I've been thinking about it a lot. I can't get excited about it." Her eyes search the floor for answers.

"Okay." I think for a moment. "When you applied, what was it that was most exciting for you?"

She takes a deep breath and lets it out loudly. "I had been in my role for two years. I hadn't been promoted yet. I wanted to be a CEO someday. I thought I'd follow the recipe. Go to the best B-school I could get into. Maybe go into consulting for a couple of years. Then relaunch at a higher level. Maybe lead product management at a smaller company. Do the start-up thing. Then see what happens."

"Is that what you want?"

"I thought so. But no." She looks up. For all her wavering, that part is clear. I nod, waiting for her to continue.

"Turns out I like my job here."

. I raise my eyebrows. "Is that a problem?"

"Well, it's great. It's just that, part of me feels like I'm settling. I feel I could do more."

I smile, exhale a bit. There it is.

More.

"And part of me is tired of running. I've been chasing something my whole life. Always more and more and more. I never really stopped to ask why."

"Okay, so, now you're slowing down a bit and asking yourself what you really want. Does that sound right?"

"Turns out I'm happy enough with my life here at LinkedIn." She is now meeting my eyes, but she still seems pained.

"Okay, great. Have you told your parents?" We have had lots of conversations about the incredible expectations of her parents. Even though she is twenty-five, they are very much part of her life and her decision making. Her parents have always dreamed of her going to Harvard.

"Oh, yeah... there's that. Turns out that Harvard is not even the hardest part. In fact, it's not even a thing at the moment. My life really is a mess right now."

I nod and wait for her to continue.

"I have this friend, Aisha, from work, and she has a friend from college. I've been hanging out with him. He's getting his residency in Palo Alto. He's funny, he's nice to me..." She trails off, staring at the wall.

"Ah, you found a doctor boy. Just like your parents wanted!" I'm joking, trying to lighten things up. We have covered this topic before. Anitya's parents have been sending her resumes for "nice doctor boys" since she was a senior in college.

"Kind of. His name is Jackson."

"Yeah?" In her face I see the answer to my next question. "What part of India is he from?"

"Nashville," she smirks. I let out a chuckle.

"Woah." The gravity of the situation is starting to take hold. I wince. Her parents are from Mumbai. They had moved to the States nearly thirty years ago. They dress in western clothing. They have become proud Americans. They go to high school football games, eat pizza, and they joined the local gym. Their Indian accents are still there, but only slightly. But they are still very traditional about some things. They are Hindu. They want Indian grandchildren.

"Have you told your parents that part?"

She nods, almost imperceptibly.

"That's huge news. How did it go?" I am remembering when I first met my own in-laws. I can feel the tension.

"I thought my dad would be upset and my mom would be neutral, at least. But she's the one freaking out. She's telling me to break it off with him. Telling me to end it or I'm not part of the family anymore. End it, or I'm not her daughter." Anitya's eyes flash with anger.

"Geez! Oh no. I'm sorry."

"I like my job here. And..." she sighs a deep sigh that has been welling up for fifteen years. "I love him. Jackson is the only person that has actually ever cared for me. For who I really am. He sees me."

We sit in silence for a long time.

"It sounds like you know what you want."

She takes a deep breath and closes her eyes. She takes another deep breath and opens them.

"I'm not sure that helps."

## Bubby

My friend Nick's family once had a parakeet named Bubby. His daughter Maddie, who was twelve at the time, loved animals of all types. Cats. Dogs. Rabbits. Every furry creature from Animal Planet. She wanted to be a veterinarian. She especially loved Bubby. Bubby lived in a medium-sized cage in the corner of Maddie's room. Bubby would bob his head when Maddie played music. He would eat sunflower seeds from Maddie's hand through the cage. If she put her ear very close, he would give her a little nibble. He would chirp extra loudly if he heard birds outside the window in the trees.

Maddie had a big heart—she still does. She felt bad that Bubby was in a cage and all the other birds were free to explore. She wanted Bubby to be able to fly. On the weekends, when she had others around to help, she would open the door to Bubby's cage. She enlisted the entire family to watch, to ensure all the windows and doors were closed. She even put notes on each door so no one would forget. She wanted to create a safe place for Bubby to fly around.

She sat outside the cage and encouraged Bubby to fly. "Come on, Bubby. Come on, fly around. Come on. You can do it! You're free!"

Four years of weekends. Four years of opening the cage. Four years of encouragement. Not once did Bubby leave his cage.

Not once did Bubby choose to fly.

## Understand the *External* Systems That Drive You

Our lives are governed by the systems that surround us. Our family, our schools, our churches, our society. Each one has its own set of norms, expectations, pressures. From an evolutionary perspective, being part of a group has kept us alive, kept us safe. But it comes with a tax.

We have to play by the unwritten rules of the group we're in. Staying within the rules helps us feel safe. Breaking the rules can cause us pain.

In Japan, there's a saying: "The nail that sticks out will get hammered back in."

Sometimes we belong to many groups, and the rules clash. Sometimes we want to leave one group and join another. These changes can be challenging, as they tear at the very constructs of our reality.

What systems are governing your life? When you make a decision, who are you *really* trying to please? What are the benefits that your systems are providing? Are there any systems that have outlived their usefulness?

Understanding the external systems that surround us helps us understand the choices we're making. It helps us more deeply understand the pain (or joy) we sometimes feel. This understanding can lead us to a wider variety of choices. It can lead us to a sense of personal freedom.

We may even learn to stop chasing the things we think might someday make us happy and just start chasing happiness for its own sake.

We might just leave the cage of our habits and try to fly.

Forget safety.

Live where you fear to live.

**RUMI**

# 5

# IT'S JUST SCIENCE

"HEY, DICKHEAD."
   I look around, confused.
   "Yeah, I'm talking to you, douchebag."
   We're on the school bus at night, coming back from a cattle-judging event. Somehow, I'm taking an agriculture class as a freshman in high school. It's one of the few electives available. There's no AP Physics here. I'm going to the smallest school in Kansas—sixteen kids in my entire grade. I have zero interest in Ag, but the only other electives are home economics or metal shop. I've grown up here, but I'm a stranger. I'm a ghost in my own body.

   Cal Vondril is at the front of the bus, taunting me. It's a two-hour bus ride. He's relentless. The teacher, a mountain of a man, is a few rows ahead of him, staring ahead blankly at the endless blacktop in front of us, oblivious. Or maybe he's asleep. Maybe he doesn't care. Maybe he agrees with Cal.

   I'm different. I don't belong here. I don't wear Wranglers. I don't care for horses. I don't want to take over the farm from my father, or work as an auto mechanic, or sell insurance to farmers. I don't want to be here.

I look around. Most of the upperclassmen can't be bothered. They're sleeping. Then there's Mike. Mike is my best friend. Well, in that way that he's my best friend, but his best friend is Marcus, his older cousin. I'm the third wheel. Still, he's the best I've got. He clearly hears Cal. I make eye contact with him, looking for support, looking for a lifeline. He turns away, looks out the window.

Cal has challenged me to a fight.

"Do you want to do something about it?" This has been going on for a very long time. It happens in the hallways at school. It happens in class. It happens in the parking lot.

I sometimes think maybe it's my own fault. I speak too much in class. I volunteer to do the solo in choir. I wear the wrong clothes. I have the wrong hair.

I have dark thoughts. The darkest thoughts. That special teenage cocktail of hormones, anger, frustration, isolation, and loneliness is raging. Inside, body and mind are already engaging in a full-scale assault.

I don't want to fight Cal. I'm afraid.

It's not Cal I'm afraid of. I want to get him alone, out in the country, away from all these other eyes. Away from any support he might have in this droning bus.

I'm not afraid of getting hurt. I'm afraid of the darkness that has taken over my body. I'm afraid that if I let myself engage, all the rage and isolation will break past that safe inner barrier. Every drop of confusion and frustration and loneliness will spill over in a giant wave. I will not stop. I cannot stop.

I will kill him.

I don't mean in an abstract or casual way, the thing you say to the older sister who has used your toothbrush for the fourteenth time. I've thought about it. A lot. I've planned it. I've imagined the look on his face. I've chosen the open field with the dirt-moving project underway. I've seen the bulldozer that will hide his body eight feet deep. I've readied my story and steeled my resolve for talking with the county sheriff.

The darkness in my mind is a thousand times worse than the taunting.

I play it forward. A month. A year. A lifetime.

I can see ahead and I know the darkness won't be quenched by taking his life. It will multiply. Even if I get away with it, the black thoughts and memories will be there, gnawing at me. Forever.

There's no place to hide.

I decide killing Cal is not the path to peace. Still, I fantasize about it when I'm lonely or angry, which happens more than I'd like.

A new thought takes its place. It's one that will tempt me every day for nearly two years with its own special brand of darkness. One that I have no answer for. One that will cause the suffering to end. One that might just give me peace.

I won't kill Cal.

I will kill me.

## The Body

The amygdala is two almond shaped clusters in our brains. One of its functions is to constantly be on the alert for danger, for threats. Its job is to keep us alive. It has an itchy trigger finger. Like the evening news, the amygdala is wired to notice and prioritize the one percent of things in life that are dangerous— that might kill us.

We also have two nervous systems that act in tandem like a teeter-totter. One is on while the other is off, like the accelerator and the brakes on a car. They're both useful and needed. These systems have evolved with us, over millennia. If we want to have more control over our bodies, we need to learn to regulate them on purpose. When we can settle the body, we can have a better chance of settling the mind.

Imagine we're sitting around a campfire at night, a hundred thousand years ago. A stick snaps behind us in the woods. Instantly, our "fight or flight," the sympathetic nervous system, is activated. We jump up. Immediately, our heart races, pumping blood and oxygen frantically to our major muscle groups. The stress hormones adrenaline and cortisol flood our bodies. Our blood even gets stickier, to keep us from bleeding out if we get injured.

We are ready to fight the tiger in the dark. Or run for our lives.

In our modern world, this system allows us to quickly step back from a bus that is careening around a corner at us. Our amygdala is on high alert, searching for any danger that might harm us. This is genius. This is how we have stayed alive. Great if we want to fight a tiger.

But today, we're triggered by that angry email from a customer. Our kids making noise in the other room while we're trying to concentrate on a video conference call. Traffic. A taunting teenager. Getting performance feedback. Giving performance feedback.

Our bodies are constantly triggered into fight or flight. We develop an overly negative view of the world due to our amygdala. We've been physically conditioned to have a negativity bias. We see the world as far more dangerous and negative than it really is.

The other system—"rest and digest," or the parasympathetic nervous system—is the opposite. It turns on slowly. It flushes the cortisol and adrenaline from our bodies. It sends blood and oxygen to our digestive systems. It allows us to sleep.

Have you ever woken up, startled, in the middle of the night? Maybe you heard a noise and panicked, wondering if it's an intruder, or your sleepwalking two-year-old about to climb the bookcase. You're awake in an instant, on high alert, heart pounding. Then you realize it's the cat. Gizmo has been playing with the things on your dresser and has finally managed to knock the framed family photo of your Hawaii vacation onto the floor. You shoo the cat out into the hallway, shut the door, and lay back down. Except your heart is still pounding and you can still feel the adrenaline coursing through your veins. Twenty minutes later, forty minutes later, you finally fall back asleep, unharmed.

Your amygdala is smugly happy, having done its job once more.

It has kept you alive.

## Frozen

I'm frozen.

I'm standing onstage in front of three hundred people, and eight thousand more are watching by video remotely. My team and I have the keynote slot at the company all-hands meeting, talking about how we incorporate member feedback into our product development. Seventeen minutes. The CEO has just introduced me and handed me the clicker. The lights pointing toward the stage are incredibly bright. I introduce myself and the topic.

Then my mind wanders away on a fishing trip, leaving me here alone, standing onstage awkwardly with the bright lights, eight thousand pairs of eyes trained on me.

I have no clue what to say next.

I've done the homework. I came yesterday to do the rehearsal. Stood onstage, looked at the cameras past the lights, breezed through my presentation. Made jokes with the comms team. Calm like a hammock on the beach under a palm tree.

I'm an experienced public speaker. I've done this a million times. This is what I do. This is my jam. For unknown reasons, in this moment, I'm frozen.

My mind has not gone blank. My mind has twenty-three thoughts all at once.

The loudest one says, "Wait, what? Why is *this* happening?"

I can feel the lizard brain rushing to the front of the line. If I wait two more seconds it will start screaming and take over.

Instinctively, I take a deep breath, audible to all eight thousand viewers, and exhale slowly.

The lizard brain sits down. The systems have been rebooted. The lights come back on. I remember why I'm here. My presentation continues as planned. My three-second pause was only a blip, but it lasted forever.

Later, after the meeting, one of my friends on the team congratulates me and reflects: "It was so cool how you demonstrated taking a deep breath and getting centered before starting."

Um. Yeah, that *was* cool.

## Enneagram

I've just taken another one of those online tests. I've taken more than I can remember. Myers–Briggs, AVA, Insights, 5 Dynamics, DISC, StrengthsFinder, the ACT, the SAT, the ASVAB, the Stanford-Binet IQ test. Each one cracks the door open a little further, giving a few more insights into my constant search for how I compare to others, where I fit in.

Who am I?

Here's a sample of what I know so far. I'm an ambivert that trends toward introversion. This means that while I'm comfortable speaking or performing in front of people, when I need to recharge, I prefer to be alone. My idea of personal hell is going to a party where I don't know (or vibe with) anyone. Even with groups of people I do know, I prefer to have deeper conversations with two or three over the whole evening, rather than lots of surface conversations with a wide variety of people.

I'm sensitive to structure. My internal systems are in sync with time. I almost always know what time it is, regardless of whether or not I'm wearing a watch. If someone says they're going to be a few minutes late, I assume that means three. Not five. I start and end meetings on time. It's a deeply held value: do what you say you're going to do. The downside is that sometimes there's a really good conversation that's happening and time is running out. I can't help myself. We'll end on time and pick up the conversation at another point.

I know that I'm a big-picture guy, a systems thinker.

I'm great at the details the first time through, as we're building something. But after that, I get bored easily, become disengaged, and start to look for something new.

I know what my IQ is, what percentile of the population I fall in. I know how I stack up.

I've been taking these tests now for twenty-five years, each one providing more clues for my investigation.

Something's different about this one. I take the Enneagram as part of a work project. It takes twenty minutes. A few weeks later I get back a thirty-page report. It seems to tell my life story, like it's been reading my diary. My wife decides to take the same test, so we can share and compare. I like it so much I buy two more books on the subject. I spend hours reading more on the internet. I listen to podcasts, searching, constantly searching, for more clues.

While many of the other tests are focused on how I show up to others, the Enneagram digs into why I do what I do. It lays me bare.

Reading these books, these descriptions of the nine archetypes of people, I have two major realizations that leave me humbled and slightly embarrassed.

I have a lot of interests—photography, music, work, cycling, golf, travel, puzzles, games—anything where I can compete. I had viewed myself as a unicorn. I'm the only one like me.

In my mind, all my hobbies and interests were a way to express my talents, to let my inner creativity shine. They were each a unique expression of my inner self.

My identity. My unicorn-ness.

This test, this interpretation, is less excited, less complimentary of all my many activities. Instead, it is pouring light on the fact that I'm not able to sit still. I'm not able to be with my pain, so I run away to the next shiny thing, pushing the discomfort deep inside, never to be dealt with. Hiding from it and instead staying busy, like a heroin addict looking for their next fix. My many interests do not reflect my great capability, they reflect my great cowardice. My fear of handling discomfort.

And there's more: while there are differentiators, twenty-nine percent of the population shares the same archetype as me—Enneagram 7. Wait, what? Twenty-nine percent of humans also operate this way?!

I'm not a unicorn.

I'm like other people. I'm like *a lot* of other people.

I'm not sure how I feel about that.

## Why Am I Bitching?

"How was your weekend?"

I've been away at a spiritual seminar, sort of like a retreat. It's a chance to recharge, to get quiet, to connect with old friends. It's typically a three- or four-day commitment. I travel a lot with my work, which puts pressure on my wife and our family. She's been patient, but I've come to see the strain.

I get to reconnect and regroup. She's at home with the kids, trying to hold things together, sometimes just trying to hold on. She has taken care of things. She has made it easy for me to go. She has put her own life and plans on hold so I can do this. I am appreciative, but I am also unaware. I'm still focused on my own story.

When she asks her question about my weekend, I start telling a story about how I'd had dinner with two old friends, one of whom was annoying me. He was making some life choices that were irritating to me. I went on about him, complaining about my interaction.

I can see my wife's enthusiasm start to fade, her eyes narrowing. It is not going well for me.

Sadly, it isn't until later that I realize what happened. I had just spent a great weekend away. If you asked me to rate it, I would have given it a 9.5 out of 10. So many good things happened. I had been able to recharge spiritually. I had gotten some incredible, deep insights about my relationships, about work, about myself. I connected with family members and old friends. I had even been able to do some photography in a grove of sugar maples in their full fall color while visiting a temple outside of town.

When asked how my weekend was, apparently my amygdala took over. It focused on my own story, dimming my awareness of my partner. It focused on the one thing across the whole weekend that irritated me.

The one percent.

Like the evening news, the amygdala is focused on the one percent of life that is scary, or disruptive, or irritating. Maybe that's helpful for keeping us alive in times of danger. But in this moment, coming home fresh to my harried wife, who had just spent the long weekend solo parenting, in this moment, apparently unaware of what it's like to be someone else, my amygdala is unwittingly trying to get me killed.

It isn't the first time.

## Understand the *Internal* Systems That Drive You

The life choices we make on a daily basis are tightly interwoven with our own internal systems and our guiding compass. Our bodies and minds have evolved in a way that prioritizes safety, not necessarily happiness. Our amygdala is constantly scanning our lives for threats, focused on the most dangerous one percent of our lives. On a physical level, this causes us stress, and gets in the way of making good choices. On a mental level, we have a bias toward the negative, which, left unchecked, leads us to misery.

When we understand these systems, we can learn to make different choices. We can learn to manage these systems. We can learn to calm our bodies. We can calm our minds. We can shift our thinking from pessimism to optimism.

This optimism allows us to increase the aperture of our lives.

This optimism will lead us to freedom.

## PART II

# Love
# Yourself

For ages you have run from the
pain and forfeited the ecstasy.
So come, return to the root
of the root of your own soul.

**RUMI**

# 6

# FINDING OUR TRUE SELF

I RING THE DOORBELL at Steven's house. I have driven to
Monterey to play music and hang out. It's 11 a.m. on a sleepy
Sunday. It's a typical foggy and cool Monterey morning.
A good morning for tea.

Steven opens the door.

"Hey, man!" he says, bleary-eyed.

He looks like he's still up from the night before. I'm pretty
sure he's wearing the same clothes he had on yesterday, which
he may have also worn to work on Friday. He has a huge and
silly grin on his face. I blurt out a laugh as we bro-hug.

"Dude. *What* is happenin'? What have you done?" I ask,
laughing. Clearly something is up. He looks like the dog that
has just eaten the cupcakes off the dining table.

"Oh maaaaaaan!" He's shaking his head back and forth,
looking to the sky in ecstasy. "It's so amazing!" He's speaking
very slowly, as if he's discovered fire. Finally, with holy reverence, he says:

"I found my sound!"

Steven is an extraordinary blues guitarist. He's been playing in local bands since he was in high school. He channels

Stevie Ray Vaughan, so of course we call him Stevie sometimes. Many years ago, one of his bands opened for Santana. He's the real deal. We've worked at two different companies together and have known each other for over twenty years. Playing the blues is in his veins. It's fun to play together. He's kindly tolerant of my singer-songwriter style, patiently waiting for his opportunity to drop in a solo during one of my originals. We ride mountain bikes together. Brothers from another mother.

He gets me.

The day before, a Saturday afternoon, he had been cruising around a guitar shop. Guitarists are always on the prowl. When asked by our spouses, "Just how many guitars do you really need?" the answer is, "Oh, just one more"—said with the mischievous smile of a ten-year-old that took an extra piece of cake when the aunties weren't looking.

He had found an old 1960s Fender tube amplifier in the used gear section, which then made its way back to his makeshift studio. That was at 4 p.m. The next time he looked up it was 4 a.m. The twelve hours in between were essentially an out-of-body experience. He was in the flow.

Steven has been searching for his signature sound, the combination of guitars, amps, and effects that represent his style—that represent him. Somewhere last evening he discovered this golden alchemy. Didn't stop for food. Didn't take a break. Made a quick and distracted "okay g'night" when a family member peeked in to see if he was still alive before heading to bed.

He had found his sound, something he'd been seeking for thirty years. It had always been inside of him. He knew it was there, could feel its presence. But couldn't quite manufacture the same thing externally. Until now. Here it was, a living, pulsing thing.

Steven is lucky. He has found a vehicle to communicate from this place, this deepest part of ourselves. Our essence. Our True Self.

Soul.

## We're Each Searching for It in Our Own Way

Through our hobbies, through our relationships, we're searching for something. It's in our language. When someone expresses it, we say "she really lit up," as if our True Self is a bright ball of light surrounded by the other parts of us that help us get around—the physical body, our emotions, our mind. When we're "lit up," our True Self is being seen, glowing strong enough to penetrate the outer shells.

These shells—physical bodies, emotions, minds—are critical. They help our True Self express itself. They make up our personality. They can also get in the way. They can take over our awareness: like in a rowdy conversation at the dinner table, sometimes our True Self never gets a word in. Has to just sit there and wait for things to calm down. Sometimes has to wait through entire careers, entire marriages, or even entire life-times before speaking with authority. Mostly, it's there every day, speaking softly and subtly if we listen carefully, like when we're in the shower or on a walk in the woods and get that special insight we've been looking for.

When we're fully present, our True Self gets to play. I think this is why we love our hobbies so much. When I'm mountain biking, screaming down some sweet single-track in the Santa Cruz Mountains, trying to find the perfect line, you know what I'm not thinking about? I'm not thinking about work. I'm not thinking about getting bullied when I was fifteen. I'm not thinking about the big project I have due in a few weeks or the bills I need to pay.

I'm fully present.

Remember when you first fell in love with someone and you were *so* into them? Maybe you were at dinner, enjoying pork three ways with a nice drink in your hand. When they spoke, you leaned in and the whole world disappeared.

You were fully present.

Or maybe in college you were at a party and connected with someone new. Pretty soon you were making out on the couch, and the whole world disappeared. Nothing else existed except you and that other person. Fully present.

Turns out being fully present is twice as big of a factor in our happiness as the actual activities in our lives. In other words, I could be doing something I don't really enjoy, like washing dishes at the sink. If I'm fully present while washing dishes, I'm probably going to be happier than if I were engaged in one of my hobbies but thinking about something else.

We experience our True Self when we're fully present.

Our True Self is creative, generative, joyful, light. Our minds and bodies—our amygdala—have been finely tuned, programmed to keep us alive. But happy? That's an afterthought.

If we want to be happy, deeply fulfilled, whole, we need to learn to live as our True Self.

We need to find our sound.

## Tuning In

We have so many distractions that keep us from being fully present. Television, with non-stop programming that gets more compelling every day. Our phones are a gold mine of distraction, from Facebook to Instagram to Snapchat to TikTok. Our news channels are always shouting at us, triggering our amygdala. We start to think we can't live without these things. We need them. Have to stay informed. Have to stay connected. Have to stay busy, doing, reacting.

We have our moments of connection. When we're present for a loved one. When we're hiking out in the wild, or at least in nature. When we first wake up in the morning in that liminal state between sleep and wake, it's there.

Then we check our email and it's gone. We become ghosts of our True Self.

It's not hard to tap into that deeper part of ourselves, but it does take work. It takes attention. It takes discipline. We're competing with the news, with eight seasons of *Game of Thrones* on demand, with TikTok videos.

Most practices to get centered and tap into something deeper start with the breath. Taking deep, conscious breaths calms down the fight or flight system and activates the rest and digest part of our nervous system. The body settles.

Long deep breaths in. Long deep breaths out.

One Latin word for breath is spiritus. Breath, spirit, same essence. Another is inspiro, like inspiration. It's embedded in our language. It has always been there. If we slow down and just breathe, we can tap into that deeper part of ourselves, that inspired part of ourselves—our spirit, the True Self, soul.

Beyond breathing, we can focus our attention. A simple way is to focus our attention on our breath. We just notice the breath as it comes into our body, and then leaves our body. If we want to go one step further, we can inwardly count our breaths. In one, out one, in two, out two, and so on.

Like a snow globe that has been stirred up and then placed down on a table, our mind begins to settle as well. We'll still have thoughts. Our mind produces thoughts, just like our stomach produces stomach acid—we're not likely to stop it.

It's not necessary to have our minds go completely blank. We're just looking to slow things down, to stop being a servant to our minds, to slow the flood.

When we're in this peaceful, relaxed state, breathing, focusing our attention, our minds and bodies can both begin to settle. From this place we have a chance to be fully present. A chance to be happy, creative, joyful, graceful, and compassionate. From here, we have a chance to go further on our inner journey, to experience life, consciousness, from that deeper part of ourselves.

After that conversation with my brother when I was thirteen, I started a practice that I still enjoy today. I use a sound mantra, the word HU, pronounced "hue." It's sung with joy. Long and drawn out, and repeated. Sometimes for just a few minutes. Sometimes for twenty minutes or more. Beyond the settling of the body and the mind, the sound acts like a tuning fork for that highest part of me. It connects me to something deeper. My True Self. The place where mysteries are unfolded. The world of poetry and light.

It starts with just one breath.

## 126 Yards

When my son Kameron was in high school, he was on the school golf team. We used to play together five or six times per month. We enjoyed spending time together, being outdoors, getting some exercise. We didn't take ourselves too seriously, but we are both competitive, so we were constantly trying to get better.

Earlier that year, my father had passed away. He had been my rock of stability as the world turned around me. After a rough patch of teenage angst, our relationship had taken root, blossomed. I always looked to him for validation, for those "attaboys." Now he was gone. At the time, my manager was giving me a lot of space at work. This was fine. I was an executive and I was confident managing my own responsibilities. I didn't need anything from him to lead the day-to-day business. But that meant there was no authority figure at work I could confide in, no one to seek validation from. No superior to give me an attaboy. In my spiritual life, my lifelong mentor and friend, my closest confidant, was also not available to me.

I was a ship in a storm, needing to create my own harbor.

One Sunday afternoon I am waiting for Kameron to come home so we can go play golf. When he finally returns, he is tired and wants to do something else. I am restless and decide to go by myself. I need to get out. The sun is fading as I start out on one of our favorite local courses. I have the whole place to myself. I realize that I haven't played alone for a long time, maybe five years. I mostly play with Kameron or at an occasional work outing. I don't mind the solitude—I grew up that way. There is something comforting about being alone in nature. It gives me time to enjoy the way the light streams through the trees at the bottom of the creek. I listen for the birds and tune in to their conversations.

As I come to the third hole, set near a tiny creek and surrounded by trees changing color, I scout for foxes. If you leave a sandwich in your golf cart, they're always happy to relieve you of it when you aren't looking. My restlessness is fading, and I am feeling right with the world. My dad's passing and the changes in my life have left me unsettled. But here, in the softening September light, I can simply be.

The hole is a par 3, 126 yards. I strike my pitching wedge well. In flight, the ball seems like it's on target. I'm not super-consistent at golf. Most of my shots are pretty good, but then I'll hit one that looks like I've never played before. My ball lands online with the flag. I can't see the hole itself, because there is a raised bunker blocking the view.

But I know.

I get that Full Body Yes. I am sure that the ball went in the hole.

In golf, a hole-in-one is a big deal. It's elusive. Some serious golfers go their entire lives without getting one. It's tradition that the player who shoots one "gets to" buy drinks for their foursome at the end of the round. In some places you buy drinks for the whole clubhouse. You can get your name in the paper.

On this day, I have been playing golf for twenty-five years, hundreds of rounds. I haven't played alone in years. Yet, here I am. Alone. Solitary. Just the birds and me. And the foxes. Contemplative. Close to nature. Closer to that inner sanctuary that lives within me.

I can't see it, but I know the ball is in the hole. The whole setup is perfect. This is how my life works. Playing alone, leading alone, but not feeling alone.

I shake my head, smile, and mutter, "You gotta be kidding me." I let out a long sigh. As I walk the 126 yards to the hole, the lesson begins to unfold. *This is just for* you. *How do* you *want to feel about it?* The Voice is there. I am not alone.

As the youngest of five I unconsciously and consciously looked for ways to shine brighter than my siblings. All in an attempt to win my parents' affections—especially my father's. Even as an adult I would seek this out.

Why? Why do we need this? What void are we trying to fill when we ourselves are already whole?

I imagine the scene on a normal day, playing with my son and another twosome. There would be joyous shouting and laughter, high fives and bro-hugs, some dancing around, perhaps some dramatic club dropping and posturing. There would be photos, lots of photos, to commemorate the occasion. There would be drink buying and storytelling, each golfer recounting it from their own perspective, their own lens. There would be posting online and retelling the story at work, each time an opportunity to bask in the glow of admiration from others. Each an opportunity to stroke my ego. To feel whole. To be held. To be seen.

*This is just for* you. *How do* you *want to feel about it? How do* you *want to experience it?*

Without the filter of posturing for others. Without the need to have my experience seen in the reflection of others. Is it good? Is it bad? Is it important? Is it meaningless? I'd spent my whole life seeking external validation for each of my achievements, then doubling down to have as many achievements as possible to get more validation.

*This is just for* you.

I have entered a deep calm, the kind I get after meditating for twenty minutes. Clarity.

I walk up to the green. I see the divot mark four feet in front of the hole. I walk closer and look down, inspecting the bottom of the cup. There is my ball, with my mark.

Of course.

*Of course* it happened this way. I look around. Still no one in sight. I take out my phone and snap a couple of pictures of my ball in the cup. No way to prove it. No way to share it. No dancing or posturing or posting. No one else to reflect the experience. I am by myself. Alone. Not alone.

*This is just for* you. *How do* you *want to feel about it?*

I take it all in. The light streaming through the trees. The simple beauty of nature. The constant presence of my father. The solitude. I feel held by the Universe, connected to everything.

I feel whole.

You were born with wings.
Why prefer to crawl through life?

RUMI

# 7

# THE INTERSECTION POINT

"**M**AKOTO, WHAT IS that shrine for?"

It is the summer between my junior and senior years in high school. I'm an exchange student near Osaka, Japan, living with a middle-aged couple and their two sons. The boys are both just a bit younger than me.

I have always been obsessed with Japan. At fifteen I wanted to be a ninja. I bought throwing stars and a set of nunchakus. I practiced spinning them, while watching myself in the mirror, admiring how cool I was. It was less cool when I'd occasionally drop myself to the floor by smacking myself in the back of the head.

A couple of summers before my trip to Japan I had visited my sister, who lived about five hours away in Kansas City. She took me to a museum that had a traveling Japanese art exhibit. I was enthralled. I didn't want to leave. I bought a poster of one of the pieces, a four-hundred-year-old screen, depicting an epic battle. It hung in my room at home instead of Cindy

Crawford or Farrah Fawcett. Um, yeah, no wonder the kids at school thought I was a bit different.

In my room, I'd look in the mirror (fifteen-year-old boys spend lots of time in front of the mirror) and stare deeply. I remember thinking, "Something's wrong." I looked some more.

"You're supposed to have brown eyes. You're supposed to have black hair. This isn't right!"

During my junior year, my guidance counselor called me into his office. I was the new kid. I had changed schools to escape the bullying. To get a fresh start. It was working. I was happy. Thriving. He let me know that there was a scholarship contest. They would pick two winners from each state. The winners would spend the following summer in Japan. I took the brochure home and read every word as if it had been sent by a new lover.

My father was less enthusiastic. Summer is the busiest time of year on the farm. Wheat harvest. It's "go" time, sunup to sundown, six days a week. Farmers only get paid at harvest time. You can work like a dog all year long, but if you don't bring in the crop, you don't get paid. Dryland farming is not for the faint of heart. You have to be a gambler. There are a hundred things that can go wrong. Mechanical breakdowns. Insects. Fire. The wrong mix of fertilizer. The wrong seed variety. Plant too late or too early. And then, weather. Most conversations start with commentary on the weather, usually about rain. Rain in Kansas sometimes comes with hail. Farmers spend half their lives praying for rain. The other half praying for it to stop. They rely on their sons to help. They are not planning on their sons disappearing during "go" time.

I was wide-eyed and had big dreams. I had won the contest and had the golden ticket in my hand.

My father loved his son. What was he going to do? What sacrifice was he going to make so I could realize my dream?

This question didn't even cross my mind until I became a father myself many years later.

In Japan, my host parents pick me up at the train station. The station is tightly packed, thousands of people streaming in every direction like an anthill. I am the only one with light hair.

I spend a couple of weeks going to school with my host brothers. Everyone is friendly, but our language skills keep a distance between us. I want to play baseball on the school team. Nope. Not allowed. I enjoy exploring the city on my bike after school and on the weekends. I sneak into a pachinko parlor one day and win thirty dollars. I return the next day and lose thirty dollars. I don't go back.

Everything is new. Foreign. Exciting.

I marvel at the situation. A kid from rural Kansas living in the middle of Japan. "What's this all about?" I wonder. "What are the odds?"

What's the point?

I have an immediate bond with my host mother. Her English is not as strong as the other three, so I have to work harder to learn Japanese to communicate with her. I am there during the end of their school year. During "hell week," the boys' final exam time, I am home with okaasan (mom) for a week or two by myself. I go grocery shopping, watch her prepare meals, and tag along as she runs errands. Every morning, she stops at a tiny shrine she has built on top of a dresser in the corner of one of the tightly packed rooms. She lights incense, carefully places a fresh piece of fruit, bows her head with hands pressed together, and says a quick prayer.

Toward the end of the summer, I ask my host brother about the shrine.

"Makoto, every morning okaasan goes to that little place in the corner." I'm speaking half in Japanese and half in English for the words I don't have vocabulary for.

"What place?" He looks up from his book. He's always studying. Always reading.

"Over there in the corner." I motion. "She lights incense. She prays." I'm pantomiming the actions. Thankfully, a look of understanding lights his face.

"Ah, yes. I understand." He pauses. He's trying to speak mostly in English. He's preparing to be an exchange student to the U.S.—to Kansas!—and he substitutes Japanese words when he doesn't have the vocabulary. There's something else about his pause. He's searching for more than the vocab. He's being reflective in a way I haven't seen before from him.

"Before Naoki and I were born, okaasan had another baby. A baby girl." He pauses again, winces.

"She didn't live."

I take it in. I have a flash of understanding. *Now* it makes sense.

I have The Full Body Yes. A rush of knowing floods my insides. I nod, eyes wide. The mystery I have carried all this time is settled.

I ask a clarifying question to be sure.

"Makoto, when, exactly, was that?" He furrows his brow, thinking, and tells me. A few months before I was born.

Yep, that's what I thought.

That little girl, the one who would have black hair and brown eyes. The one that didn't make it.

That was me.

## Would You Do It for the Money?

It is 2016. I have been in my role as VP of customer operations for four years. It is my dream job. And yet, I am restless, searching for growth, searching for something new. I have never had the same role for more than two years. I have been at companies for ten years, but never in one role for that long. I have my dream job and can't imagine leaving LinkedIn. Yet, here I am, curious, taking the call.

The recruiter on the phone is pitching me a role. Chief operating officer. It is a hard role to come by and often not a fit for someone with my experience. But this one is perfect. I am just what they are looking for. It is a chance to be part of the executive staff at a rocketing start-up. They need me. They want me. My ego is intrigued, listening, ready to impress. The job is in a different city, two states away—one I have no desire to live in. My daughter has just started high school. I'm pretty sure she wouldn't speak to me for a long time if we moved. I'm telling the recruiter no, shutting the door on my ego. She is very good at her job. She makes one last attempt.

"*Okay*, I hear you. But before you say no, understand that this is going to be the next Uber. It's a unicorn on a rocket ship. We're recruiting execs from Google, Apple, and others from the who's who list in the Valley. So, just take a few days to think about it. And really, think about this: *would you do it for life-changing money?*"

Ugh. Damn it.

There it is. The choice. The choice between selling your soul and following your heart. Between what we think everyone else wants us to do and what we know to be true. Between ego and our True Self.

It sounds so simple when you're detached from it, when it's someone else's decision. We're so easily distracted from our destination. Like Odysseus, we chart a course, confident in our outcome. Then, the sirens call us. We're enchanted by their sweet song. We can hear nothing else. The next thing we know we're crashed on the rocks, achieving everything we ever wanted, except the happiness we craved in the first place.

I spend the next few days mulling over the age-old question: *what would I really do if I won the lottery?* Whether that's the SuperLotto or the start-up jackpot. What would I really do if I didn't have to work for money? It's a useful question to regularly ask, regardless of your circumstances. "If I could do anything, what would I do?"

There's a Japanese concept called ikigai, where your sweet spot lies at the intersection point of four circles, each representing one of the following: What you love to do. What you're good at. What the world needs. What someone will pay you for.

How many doors of possibilities would open if we didn't need to worry about the "what someone will pay you for" circle?

Music. Art. Photography. Poetry. Paths not taken because there is no dependable financial stream. I once wanted to move to New York to become a singer, and I never did it, largely because I was worried about the financials.

I do the math. At the end of four years (a typical vesting period for stock grants), assuming I had walk-away money, I'd still be in my early fifties—too young to retire, too restless to just garden or play golf every day.

What would I *really* do if I didn't have to work for money?

Maybe this was a chance to scratch that artistic itch? But did I really want to turn one of my hobbies into a job?

I decide my lottery job will be at the ikigai intersection of goodness—and I am becoming more clear on what that is for me. If I could do anything without worrying about financial risk and still meet all the other ikigai boxes—what I'm good at, what the world needs, what I love to do—then it would be working with companies to help them be more conscious.

If companies were more conscious, they would treat their customers better. There would be more integrity and trust in the world. If companies and their leaders were more conscious, they would treat their employees better. There would be less trauma and stress. There would be more healing. More creativity. People could be whole. We wouldn't need to think of our work life as "bad" and the rest of our lives as "good."

We can bring compassion into everything we do at work, not just because it makes others feel better, but also because it's a better strategy for success. The research bears this out. We just haven't quite caught up to it in practice yet. We can help employees find their True Self. Help them find their sound. In doing so, the company can be more successful as well.

During this inquiry—this searching for the answer to "What do I do next? How can I live my life's mission?"—I have a happy realization. I am already in the best position possible to make change, to have impact, like it had been planned this whole time. Because of my unique set of experiences, skillsets, and interests. Because of who I am at LinkedIn. Because of who LinkedIn is in the world. I don't need to leave to go somewhere else.

Without fully knowing, I have been working toward this moment for my entire career. Every experience, every struggle and failure and learning and win have all led me to where I am standing now. After twenty-five years, it all makes sense. Now I have a chance to bring my whole self to work.

I stay in my operations role, but I raise my hand and volunteer to be the executive sponsor of our mindfulness program. At this point, we don't have one, really. We pull together a group of passionate volunteers and set out to create an industry-leading program. I start leading meditation sessions at work. I come out as a meditator. I start to find the language that will make all of these things feel natural, appropriate for the work environment. Blending these two worlds together in a seamless way. I start to spend more and more of my time on this side hustle. It is such a great outlet. Such a pure expression of who I really am.

A couple of years later, Jeff Weiner, our then-CEO, gives the commencement address at Wharton. His number one piece of advice on how to be successful in life, how to be successful in business? Be compassionate. He goes public with his commitment to compassion. There is a vulnerability here. It is powerful. The next couple of times Jeff is on TV, this is all the reporters want to talk about. They ask him one question about our business, and ten questions about compassion.

I think, "Okay, it's time. It's time for us to invest in this. It's time for us, for me, to get serious. To commit. If we're going to send fifteen thousand employees back to their desks with the message that compassion is the number one thing they can do to be successful... do they know what that means? Do *we* know what that means?"

I make a pitch. We fine-tune it. There is a lot of support. A lot of trust. A few months later I have a new title and a new career. Head of mindfulness and compassion programs. We can help mainstream mindfulness. We can operationalize compassion. We can infuse compassion into everything we do as a company: how we build products, how we sell to customers, how we treat each other.

There is a slight catch. I have to let go of my ego. No potential COO role. No more VP title. I need to let all of that go.

Thirty years ago, when I was trying to decide who I was going to be in the world, I had thrown my hands into the sky and said, "I don't know. What am I supposed to do?" I had gotten The Full Body Yes. And it came with a message, a message that didn't really make sense for most of my career. One that has been rattling around inside, like a spare part not fully attached. Finally, after all these years of thinking about it, I am going to live that message and go Full Ikigai.

"Maybe you can change work from the inside out."

## Our True Self Is the Deepest Part of Us

We're more than our minds. More than our emotions. There's a deeper part of us. It is our True Self. That part of us that is limitless. That knows.

Pure energy.

Soul.

A spark of the Divine.

Our higher selves.

There are as many ways to describe it as there are people on earth. It is up to each of us to name it, to put a mental model around it so we can try to understand. Really, to describe it at all brings an unfair limitation.

It just is.

When we're able to view life from this perspective, the perspective of our True Self, it changes everything. We don't need to chase external validation. We don't need to chase money or titles. We don't need to chase after anything that's outside of ourselves.

We realize that we are already whole.

We can then decide for ourselves what truly gives us joy. What truly allows us to express our creativity, to grow, to thrive.

When have you felt most "at home"? Doing what activity? With whom? When do you feel like you're at your very best, living with purpose?

What's your personal mission in life?

When we realize that there's a deeper part of us, our True Self, it comes with another realization.

Everyone else has a True Self.

When we can see it in ourselves, we can start to see it in others.

Your task is not to seek love,
but merely to seek and find all
the barriers within yourself
that you have built against it.

**RUMI**

# 8

# BE YOUR
# OWN LIGHTHOUSE

"**A**RE YOU REALLY playing music again this year?"

My friend asks me this about a month away from our neighborhood block party in San Jose. We shut down the block to cars, pulling tables and chairs into the middle of our quiet street. The kids play basketball. Someone arranges to have firefighters and their firetruck come. If there's not a drought going on, the firefighters will open up one of the hydrants for the kids to play in. There is a cornhole tournament, endless barbeque, and a fair amount of drinking.

And music. Vincent and I normally set up a little makeshift stage on his porch and play guitars and sing.

"I was planning to. Why?"

"Well..."

"What is it?"

"I'm not sure that you should this year."

I can feel my face getting hot. "Why's that?"

"It's just that... I don't know if people are that into it."

"Really?" I am starting to get jumpy.

"Yeah. Last year lots of people left the area you were in and went to go drink in peace somewhere else."

That feeling in my stomach comes on suddenly, like I am on a heaving sailboat in giant waves that make me feel small.

I have been excited about playing music. I have been starting to practice, trying to find more songs that people know the words to, so they can sing along. I googled "best party songs for acoustic guitar" and have been making my way through the list.

I am liking my friend less and less, and he isn't done yet.

"Yeah, I mean, honestly? I don't know if you're that good."

Ouch. Seriously? I stare at my hands, the blood rushing into my ears. My jaw tightens.

"Yeah. And . . . does it always have to be about you? Why do you feel the need to be onstage all the time anyway?" He put on a mocking bully's voice. "*Look at me! Look at me!*"

I put my guitar back in its case. I shut down my search windows. I am not excited about the block party anymore. In fact, now I am thinking about ways to get out of going. I don't want to see those people. I can't face them. Not now. Not now that I know they think I'm terrible. Not now that I know I've been making a fool out of myself for years.

Instead of practicing a few happy songs, I am filled with self-loathing. My body is twisted into an anxious mess.

I need to find a very small cave to escape into.

And my friend?

That friend is a jerk.

Somehow, I keep him around; he keeps showing up. He means well. He thinks he's protecting me, telling me secrets and truths that no one else will. He's been around a long time. He thinks he knows me better than anyone else.

That friend . . .

Is me.

It's that small, ugly voice in my head that gnaws at me, tries to shelter me from pain by inflicting pain. It's the small "no" voice, the mental equivalent of the amygdala, always pointing out the bad stuff that might hurt me. Trying to keep me safe.

It's the one that told me to just sit down instead of going to talk to the pretty girl at the bar in college.

It's the one that interjects "yeah, but..." each time someone gives me a compliment.

It's the one that tells me no matter how much I achieve, no matter how successful I am, my father won't love me the way I need him to.

I'm by myself in my home office, tears slowly creeping down my hot face.

To hell with that voice.

Luckily, I have more perspectives roaming in my mind. In addition to that inner critic, I have inner champions. If I let them, if I calm down and be still, their wisdom can be heard.

Inhale. Exhale.

Inhale.

Exhale.

Just.

Slow. Down.

My True Self is in there somewhere. It's more curious, asks more questions. It sees the full picture.

"Actually, lots of people are into your music," it tells me. "For some, you know, it's their favorite part of the evening. They ask you to play every time."

I nod, my jaw still tight.

"Remember how they like to sing along. If you don't sing, they won't sing either. They'll be afraid to. That would be a shame."

I sigh, nod again.

"Not everyone is going to hang out in the same area as you're playing. Even if John Lennon himself showed up, some would still prefer to play beer pong or tell stories as they trade whiskey shots." Yes, that's also true.

"You don't have to do this, or not do this, for anyone other than you. If you feel like playing music, if you enjoy it, then you should do it. Because other people will appreciate it. They enjoy the music. They enjoy you. You decide. Do what you want to do."

I sigh again. I feel better. I walk the dog to clear my head.

When I return, I continue my search for party songs. My three-ring songbook has grown fat. I'm up to eighty that I can play confidently. I go back to practicing.

On the night of the party, I tell my mean friend to shut the hell up. Leave him at home.

We play music on Vincent's porch for three hours. People sing along. We have a great time.

I have a great time.

## Holding It All

"I don't know what's okay to feel."

My daughter Anjali is a senior in high school. We're in the middle of the COVID-19 pandemic. She's mourning the loss of her senior year. Graduation. Prom. She is the captain of the lacrosse team—they had been favored to win the league this year after losing every single game her freshman season. The senior farewell rally. The senior trip. This should be her time. Her glory days.

All of it, gone.

In the beginning there had been hope. "Maybe we'll still have prom." Like a balloon slowly leaking air, each event is canceled. Quarantined. Stuck inside. Nothing to do. No one to see. Now even leaving for college is uncertain. Everything in life is uncertain.

There is no point in waking up before noon. Hard to get excited about art projects or learning a new song on the piano.

Hard to get excited about anything. She sinks deeper and deeper inside herself, stuck in a fetal position in bed.

Then George Floyd is killed in Minneapolis. Four hundred years of racial tension boil to the surface. News cycles fill with chaos. With rage. There is a feeling in her stomach: *I must do something.* On the day that was to be her graduation ceremony, instead of walking across the stage in her cap and gown, she and her friends make signs. They post their plans online. They find their way to our little downtown area to demonstrate. Others hear the call. They are joined by sixty more. The next day there are nearly two hundred. They are peaceful. Respectful.

Determined.

They are on the cusp of adulthood, preparing to enter a world that is newly undefined. Uncertain. A world they are watching unfold, unravel. A world on fire. A world they do not want to inherit.

Their energy and frustration has an outlet.

Thinking about something else, *someone* else, giving energy toward a bigger cause, lifts Anjali's spirits. She has a purpose. She gets fired up. She makes more signs. She reads more articles. We have deeper discussions at the dinner table about the world.

She is alive.

During this time there are also graduation parties. A parade of cars with graduates, smiling parents and teachers waving from the streets, wishing they could give the kids something different. A different type of graduation. A different type of world. There are quiet gatherings with cake and balloons and pictures.

There is much discussion online about what to post on social media. Racial and social injustice rule the headlines. We should only be posting about that topic. No posting about graduation or parties or celebrations. It is appropriate for the discussion on racial justice to be front and center and focused.

True mindfulness is
having an awareness
of the present moment
without judgment.

And Anjali is conflicted.

"I don't know what's okay to feel!"

How can she feel happy for herself when injustice rules? How can she celebrate this milestone with her friends, laughing and enjoying each other, when other people are getting teargassed and shot? How can she feel joy when others are suffering?

Love for all of life. Love for ourselves. These are hard to see in the storm.

True mindfulness is having an awareness of the present moment without judgment. It's having an awareness of how we feel. All of it. We're complicated. Our lives are not filmed in monochrome.

We're capable of holding space for it all. There's room for us to celebrate one part of our life while another part is falling apart. We're naturally programmed for negativity. We have to work extra hard to balance pessimism with optimism, with gratitude.

When we feel joy, it strengthens us. It makes us more capable.

We're not sugarcoating the hard things. We're not looking away. We're not ignoring the vast sea of problems in the world and in our own lives.

We're also not consumed by them. We're not held down by their weight.

When we celebrate the good things, it makes us more resilient. It makes us whole. And in that wholeness, we are more masterful in dealing with life's terrors. It strengthens our resolve to work against the darkness, to right the wrongs. We are more alive and present to serve.

The light and the dark are always among us.

Within us.

We must give the light a chance.

## I Love You

Our inner critics rage inside of us. They think they're help-ing, keeping us safe. But our confidence, our happiness, are the least of their concerns. They are bullies. It is up to us to stand up and do something about it. If the inner critics, like the amygdala, are focused on the one percent of life that might put us in danger, it is up to us to balance the scales with all the other things that are true.

If we ever hope to build our muscle for showing compas-sion to others, it helps to first show compassion to ourselves. If we don't love ourselves, how can we love others?

Let's start with something that's both incredibly simple, and, for some of us, incredibly hard.

Put your hand on your heart. Take a deep breath. Feel the soothing touch of your hand on your heart. Continue this deep breathing as you read this. Seriously, do it. Put your hand on your heart right now. Recognize that you are here. This may be obvious, but I mean your attention, your awareness is here, in your body, with your hand on your heart. Inhale. Exhale. Sloooow down.

Inhale.

Exhale.

Now, say your name, and then "I love you."

Yep, I know, it might feel weird. Do it anyway. Do it again.

"(Name), I love you."

Let the words sink in. Don't try to deflect. Don't laugh it off. Don't make it into a joke.

"(Name), I love you."

If you're still reading this and you haven't tried it yet, it's time to give it a try. Say it unconditionally. Without judgment. Without a filter.

"(Name), I love you."

Let go of your opinions. Let go of your fear. Let it all go and just be here. Now.

"(Name), I love you."

Smile and take a deep breath.

"(Name), I love you."

Now smile again, close your eyes, and just be with yourself. Listen.

## How Do I Compare?

We're high performers. We've been trained to be. It started early. Very early. I remember visiting our neighbors when our babies were just months old. Even then, there was a noticing, a comparing of achievements. "Is Caleb sitting up yet?" "Dana was only five months old when she started sitting by herself." Then it's crawling, walking, first words.

As parents we say to ourselves and our spouses, "Each one is on their own journey. Each will develop just like they're supposed to." That's true. That's wise. And ... there's still that little voice inside of us that is noticing. The part that is a tiny bit prouder if our child is developing faster, better somehow.

We absorb this as kids. Every teacher, every adult, every interaction reinforces the idea. There are grades on tests. There are races to be run at recess. There are popular groups that we migrate toward or away from.

It starts early.

It's hard not to compare ourselves with others.

There's a positive benefit to comparing. We find a role model. We notice their good qualities and work to cultivate those qualities within ourselves. We're proud of ourselves for the growth we've had. That's helpful. That's not usually what happens.

Usually what happens is we compare ourselves with others and view any gap between us as loss, as failure.

*Tina made it to state in cross country. I barely placed in most of our local events.*

*Damien got into the University of Michigan. I'm going to community college until I figure out what I want to do.*

*Brian has gotten promoted twice. I'm still working in the same job as when we both started.*

Being a high performer is not a bad thing. Learning new skills, working hard, building a craft, expressing our creativity, getting *really good* at something. These are healthy expressions of our True Self.

Where we go off the rails is getting attached to the result. This is one of the biggest challenges in life, especially at work. How do I perform at a very high level and be at peace at the same time? The answers have always been there.

*Each kid develops at their own pace.*

*It's the journey, not the destination.*

*Money won't buy you happiness.*

It's hard to see this when we're in the middle of it.

Imagine training for a marathon. It's your first one. You've done some local 5 and 10Ks. Your buddies have convinced you to run a marathon with them. You agree. There's a twelve-week training program to adhere to. There's a diet plan. You follow both religiously. Each day you're putting in the work. You're doing your pre-run stretches and your post-run cooldowns. You do some yoga to stay limber. You watch what you eat. You replace your shoes on time. You hydrate. Every day you can feel yourself get stronger, fitter, faster. Healthier. Your mood lightens.

When you're out on a run you start to notice how the grass is getting greener now that spring is here. The trees are budding, and new leaves are growing. You're getting used to rising early. You actually look forward to waking up for the group runs at 5:45 a.m. You look forward to the sunrises. You look forward to the connections you've built with your little team. On the weekends your training plan starts calling for long runs. When you first started, you had never run more than six miles in your whole life. Now that's a normal day. The long runs are twelve miles. Eighteen miles. When you finish them, you feel a sense of accomplishment. Strong. You start to show that strength in other areas of your life.

Over the course of three months you develop a deeper understanding of your diet and how it affects your body. You know that too much sugar leaves you light-headed and irritable in the afternoons. Too much fried food leaves you feeling sleepy. You start food shopping differently. You're reading the labels for the first time. You're eating healthier. You feel better. Your inner talk track is healthier. Kinder. Your family notices. You're easier to be around.

On race day there's a strategy. You know not to start out too fast. Don't get sucked into sprinting with the people up front. Life lessons are all around you. *It's not a sprint. It's a marathon,* they say. "Yeah, literally!" you think. "Just run your own race."

You find the pace group that will run nine-minute miles. You settle in with them. By mile eighteen you'll know if you can go faster or if you'll just be hanging on. It hurts, but it feels good at the same time. You smile at the other participants along the way. You go as hard as you can.

As you round the final corner with half a mile to go, you're surrounded by cowbells and cheering fans. Your family is here to take pictures and shout encouragement from the sideline. They are beaming. They've seen the transformation in you. They've changed as well. They've been inspired by your growth. Your nine-year-old daughter is already thinking about how she'd like to run a marathon someday when she grows up.

You've done everything you could do. You've followed the experts' training plan. You've eaten the right foods. You've gotten enough sleep. You're following the strategy exactly as you planned. As you cross the finish line and throw your hands in the air, you know that you've completely maxed out your capability. You've run as fast as you can possibly run. There was nothing more you could have done. You left it all on the course. You smile a giant smile as you hold your finishers' medal, basking in the endorphins.

You did it. No one can ever take that away from you.

You did it.

In that moment, does it really matter that your buddy David finished twelve minutes ahead of you?

## Loving Ourselves Is a Big Step Toward Loving Others

Keeping score versus others as a measure of success is a strategy for misery. If you truly want to keep score, you can compare yourself with the person you were yesterday. The person you were last year. Five years ago.

Are you happier? Wiser? More loving?

In her book *Self-Compassion*, the researcher Kristin Neff calls out three main components of her title subject.[2]

It starts with mindfulness. Awareness. We typically have a negativity bias. Our amygdala is trying to keep us alive. It's busy pointing out all the things that are dangerous. All the places we've failed.

That inner critic is based on old programming. Keeping us alive versus keeping us content or happy. It's up to us to replace it. Each time we hear the whisper of the inner critic in our ear, we can stop and acknowledge what's happening. We can say, "Ah, I see you. Thank you for your feedback."

In World War II, there were Japanese soldiers posted on remote islands around the Pacific. There was little or no fighting taking place there. They were there just in case the fighting expanded to that island. When the war was over, they were forgotten. No one told them the war was over. Years went by. When people finally arrived on the island, there was a lot of explaining to do. These soldiers had played a valuable role. At some point, it was time for them to go home. They were no longer needed there. Their job was done.

We can treat our inner critic like these soldiers. We can thank it for its service. We can appreciate what it tries to do for us. The information our inner critic shares is important. The problem is that this voice is like your grumpy uncle Phil when he's had too much to drink at Thanksgiving; it's the loudest voice in the room and won't stop talking. After we acknowledge the voice for its service, for keeping us alive and safe, we can gently but firmly tell it that it's time to leave.

Like mental aikido, we can then shift our approach. We ask ourselves, "What else is true? In addition to all the negative things my inner critic is telling me, what else is true?" We usually have a long list of things that are okay or even good in our lives. There's a long list of things we can be grateful for.

Next, we realize we're not the only ones that have ever felt this way. We're not alone. Other people have let themselves down. Other people feel lost. Other people sometimes don't like themselves very much. It's not just us.

We're not alone.

Third, kindness. We need to apply the Golden Rule to ourselves. Treat ourselves the way we'd like other people to treat us. Nobody likes getting yelled at or criticized constantly. Why do we tolerate doing it to ourselves?

We need to stop it. Instead ... give yourself some kindness.

Say, "(Name), I love you."

Tune in to that deeper, True Self.

Listen.

Gratitude is wine for the soul.
Go ahead. Get drunk.

**RUMI**

# 9

# BLACK BELT
# LEVEL GRATITUDE

THERE'S AN OLD parable that goes something like this.

A young boy gets a horse for his tenth birthday. He's excited. He's always wanted a horse. His parents are so pleased to give him one. The people of his town say, "That's good!"

One of the elders, the wise man in town, says, "We'll see."

A few years later the boy is racing home and gets careless. He falls off the horse and breaks his leg. It's pretty severe. It doesn't heal properly. He will never walk the same as he did before.

He's devastated. The people of the town say, "That's terrible."

The wise man observes and says, "We'll see."

A few years later war breaks out. All of the young men in the countryside are called to war. They must leave their families and loved ones behind and report for duty, not knowing if they'll ever return. Our young man with the broken leg is rejected from the army due to his limp. He stays at home in the village while the other men go to war.

The townspeople say, "That's good!"

The wise man takes a deep breath and ponders. He says, "We'll see."

## Tim

"Knowing what you know now, would you choose this body again?"

Tim smiles a deep, wise smile and thinks about my question.

I am volunteering with my spiritual group at a community center on a Saturday morning. We are leading a workshop on dreams. My job is to be the greeter. The session has started already, and I am outside waiting for anyone who might show up late. I am standing on a second-floor walkway, overlooking the outdoor courtyard. I watch as the gymnasium doors on the first floor open and a rowdy group of young people pours out. They are having fun, laughing, joking, throwing things at each other. They are so alive, so joyful. I enjoy watching them, enjoy their presence.

One thing is different, though. They are all in wheelchairs. They have just finished playing wheelchair basketball in the gym.

One of the young men has seen our signs and rides the elevator up to see what's going on. I share a bit of what we're up to. He doesn't want to go inside, but he does want to talk. We essentially end up having the workshop together out on the walkway.

Have you ever met someone and clicked so quickly that within five minutes you're having a deep, connected conversation? That's how it goes. We have gone there. We are totally in sync. I learn that his name is Tim. He is in his early twenties. He doesn't have the use of his legs—never has. One of his arms is mostly non-functioning. He shares that his insides don't process food the same way mine do. He needs help doing nearly everything. From my very limited viewpoint, from the lens of my own life, I am looking at Tim and thinking, "Woah, that looks hard. I wouldn't wish that life on anyone."

There is something else. Tim's eyes convey a deep wisdom, a knowingness. His body may not be ready for the NFL, but the deep understanding about life that he emanates is world class. Tim knows things.

We are having a conversation about spiritual growth, the world, and how everything might work. We start talking about the role of our physical bodies in our spiritual growth. We are talking about reincarnation and musing about what happens after this body dies. After much related discussion and inquiry, I say, "Okay, Tim, let's assume reincarnation is a thing. Let's say you're in between lives, maybe meeting with your teacher about the lessons you've learned in the past, and the lessons you'd like to learn in the next life. I'm not sure if you get to choose your body, but if you *do* get to choose, knowing what you know now, would you choose this body again?"

Tim smiles and nods. We have gone there. We are both warmed by the connection. The inner search for learning is crackling with possibility. We are locked in.

He likes the question. He looks up and off to the side, pondering deeply, his lips curved in thought.

"You know, I don't think I'd choose this body again."

I nod. Yep, that makes sense.

He waves his arm toward his friends below. "But I would choose one of those."

"Wait, what?" I think. I look down at his friends, surprised, wondering if I've missed something. They are all in wheelchairs. "Really?" I ask. "Tell me more."

He understands my surprise.

"Look, with this body, I've learned so much about joy. About humility. Patience. Trust. Strength. About service. About surrender. I've learned about compassion."

He pauses and closes his eyes, basking in the things he has learned, remembering the suffering, the searching, the joy. Recalling the lessons and the hard-earned wisdom that came with each one. And now, perhaps even as a surprise to himself, saying that he would choose to do it all over again. That he is not a victim. He is grateful for this body.

"I've learned about unconditional love."

He shakes his head slowly back and forth. "And this"—he waves his arm toward me and my body—"*this* just seems like cheating."

In Tim's view, he is the strong one. I am the weak one. In Tim's view, he has come into this life to learn as much as possible. With his unique body, he is learning at a rate that is ten or twenty times the rate of people like me in my "puny, uncreative, ordinary" body.

I nod, letting the moment sink in. We smile at each other for a long time, the kind of complicated smile when you feel every emotion, heartache and joy, all at once. When you feel your own lightness and pain, as well as the lightness and pain of another. When you connect with the Universe on an inside joke. The kind of smile that needs a lifetime to explain.

I'm not romanticizing Tim's life or his strength. He has his own issues. Huge swaths of his life are a mess. The Universe has dealt him a challenging hand and, like the rest of us, he's doing the best he can with what he has. But I'm touched by our interaction.

For a long time after this conversation, I think about Tim.

I get that feeling like something in my inner machinery has cracked, has broken and been upgraded. It's been replaced by something stronger, more vulnerable, but closer to being truth. Closer to my True Self.

I start to think about my own life.

I think about the situations that have been the most challenging. With enough time, some of the emotion, some of the charge has tapered off enough for me to see things more clearly.

When I had my job eliminated three times in four years, those were dark days. I questioned everything. There were times when I was filled with anger, when I raged at the situations that didn't go my way—or at the people who made the decisions that had caused my pain. I felt a sense of deep frustration that I didn't get the promotion that was promised to me. I felt like the bull in the ring, always chasing the red cape, never getting what I wanted.

With the benefit of time, I can look back at that whole period with a fresh perspective. Now that I'm removed from the daily drama, the inferno of emotions, I can see it more objectively. *Because* things weren't going how I wanted them to, I was forced to make changes. I got very clear on who I was and what I wanted in life, what was most important to me. I charted a new course. Got coaching certifications. Started a business on the side. Took a new job that stretched me. Each step moved down a road that eventually came to an end. Each ending felt right, and started me down another new road. I followed my heart, that inner voice. That inner knowingness. It didn't feel like wasted time. I learned to trust the process, even though the process wasn't necessarily showing the results I wanted. I was happier.

When I got my coaching certification, I thought it meant I'd have a career in executive coaching. Nope, not quite it.

When I created the start-up, I thought it was my path to financial freedom and independence from Corporate America. Nope, not quite it.

When I joined another company, I thought it might be the start of a new career. Nope, not quite it.

But all of these experiences put together led me to LinkedIn. They were the building blocks that made me uniquely qualified to do the job I was hired for. Without the inconveniences, without the failures, without the internal angst about what I really wanted, I never would have done the work that led me to my dream job.

With the benefit of time, it's not hard to see how I've grown from a tough situation. It's much harder to observe something difficult in my life *right now* and be grateful for it. Tim was able to see his physical body, on his good days, as a gift.

After our conversation, I start to think about the hardest things in my life. I try to view them differently, with appreciation. With grace. With gratitude.

I start with my relationships. At the time I meet Tim, I have a manager that I don't much care for. They make me feel small. They can be a bully. I don't feel supported or appreciated. How can I be grateful? It doesn't seem like much good is coming from this.

I had asked Tim a question: "Knowing what you know now, would you choose this body?" I start to ask myself the same question. I'm not exactly sure how the Universe works, but what if I have somehow chosen this? What if, before this lifetime, I had been sitting with my teacher, my guide, and we were reviewing the lessons I learned in the last lifetime, and the lessons I was planning to learn this time. After reviewing the lessons, what if there were a choice: "Who do you want to go with you, to help you learn?"

I imagine it was like pick-up basketball and I was choosing teams. I was looking at a roster of souls that could go with me, and it was time to choose my current boss. What if I had *chosen* this boss? *Hand-picked* them to help me grow? Selected them for their unique character traits that would push me beyond my comfort zone into a place of discovery? Of learning? Of growth?

With that in mind, I start to think about what I am learning from this situation with my manager. At first, my mind resists.

It counters, "No, no, no! There's nothing good about this! They can be such a pain. No one deserves this."

With enough space, stepping back from my own drama, I can see things more clearly. I am learning every day. I have a long list.

I am learning to communicate clearly. If I don't, my boss stares at me impatiently, or jumps on any little word I say and takes us down a rabbit hole of frustration.

I am learning to stick up for myself and my team. This manager can be a bully. They will pick someone on my team and reach a lasting judgment about them, solely on one brief interaction.

I am learning to be a good manager, a compassionate manager, by observing when it doesn't go well. My manager has many strengths. People management is not one of them.

With this new view, I start to approach our meetings more positively. I become an observer. I see the mental and emotional traps before I step into them. I am able to (mostly) let go of my frustration. I break old patterns. I try new things.

As an internal signal to myself, I decide that every time I get upset with this boss about something, I will inwardly say, "Thank you." Then I will search deeper. This allows me to stay more balanced.

"Why? Why is this upsetting me?" This inquiry leads me. Often it leads me to an uncomfortable truth about myself. If I am willing to stick with it, I can see the growth that needs to take place.

Life is happening *for* me, not *to* me.

That awareness gives me a choice.

## Gratitude Is a Superpower

Remember how our physical response, our amygdala, is constantly pointing out the things that are dangerous? We tend to focus on the worst one percent of our lives. This physical system helps keep us alive and safe—physically. Happiness, our mental well-being, is not part of that equation.

Gratitude is.

Gratitude is putting a finger on the other side of the scale.

A study once found that people who keep a gratitude journal are *measurably* happier. Have *measurably* fewer physical symptoms of stress. Have *measurably* more optimism.[3] Those are pretty good outcomes. What does it take?

Each day for ten weeks, the participants in the study wrote down three things they were grateful for. That's it.

More happiness. More optimism. Less stress. Who doesn't want that?

In another study, they found that people who kept a gratitude journal are more likely to stick to their exercise routines. They are more likely to stick to the diets they've chosen.[4]

Gratitude is a superpower.

The fix is simple, but not easy.

We're stingy with gratitude for others, always focused on the one percent of the other person that frustrates or irritates us, versus the ninety-nine percent of them that is just fine. The part of them that is similar to us. We're even crueler to ourselves. When we get a performance review or a 360-degree feedback report from our colleagues, we skip over the three pages of positive feedback and obsess about the one paragraph of "could be improved" comments. When we focus on the negative, we're focused on loss. We live in fear. Fear of losing. Fear of failure. Fear of what others might think of us. Fear of rejection. We think success means minimizing those failures, minimizing those imperfections. But the fear of failure is a constant companion. It's a hole that can never be filled.

We see this focus on "what could be better" as a way to keep our edge, a way to continue to sharpen the saw, to improve. I call it pothole management. There can be a thousand miles of perfect highway with one pothole. Where does our attention go? The pothole.

Most of us have spent our entire lives conditioned with this negativity bias. I'm not saying that we should be blind to the pothole. Yes, let's fix that thing. And fast! And ... let's also celebrate the thousand miles of perfect road. Let's understand how it got to be perfect. Let's cheer the workers that kept it maintained without asking. Let's have balance.

*Let's not be blind to the ninety-nine percent of what's right.*

When we take in the whole picture, the entire one hundred percent of our lives, there's so much more that has gone right. When we take some time to celebrate what's going on in our lives, we start to re-orient our thinking. We start to appreciate the little things. We can slow down and be thankful that we're healthy. We can be thankful that we're employed. We can be thankful that we're in relationships with people we love. We can be thankful for the clean water we drink. We can be thankful for every single lesson we're learning, whether it comes in a form that we wanted, or whether it's been a challenge for us.

This orientation toward gratitude opens us up to possibility. It opens us up for growth. It opens us up for creativity and out-of-the-box thinking. We become better at our relationships. We become better at our jobs. We become better at life.

Happier. More optimistic. Less stressed.

How do we reorient our lives? It takes more than intention.

I appreciate this quote from James Clear, who wrote the book *Atomic Habits*: "You do not rise to the level of your goals, you fall to the level of your systems."[5] While I love the book and its modern context, the concept is ancient. Clear has adapted a thought from the ancient Greek poet Archilochus, who said, "We don't rise to the level of our expectations, we fall to the level of our training." And even before that, Archilochus probably borrowed or relearned the concept from other teachers before him.

For my own life, here's an example at work. One of my goals is to eat less sugar. I have a huge sweet tooth, but my body doesn't appreciate it. So I try not to keep ice cream in the house, because I am, essentially, powerless against it. That's my system. My wife once threw a birthday party for me that included pie and ice cream. We had three full pies and several tubs of ice cream left over. I hate waste! I love ice cream. For the next twelve days I ate pie and ice cream once or twice per day. It was amazing! And . . . it was not what I was trying to do.

*My life had fallen to the level of my system, my training. It had not risen to the level of my intention, my goals, my expectation.*

We are creatures of habit. Inertia is often the strongest force in our lives. If I'm fifty years old, it's taken me fifty years to become the way I am. Everything I do is shaped by the choices of my past. Doing something different takes energy. It's physics: *An object in motion stays in motion in the same speed and in the same direction unless acted on by an unbalanced force.*

It's going to take time. Making change, any change, is hard. We need to help ourselves every way we can. Intentions are powerful, and a necessary first step. Recognizing where inertia is taking us and being conscious about putting helpful systems in place allows us to make real change. If you want to boost your gratitude, there are systems you can try for yourself. Here are a few.

### The gratitude buddy

The buddy system is very powerful. Get someone to join you in your quest. Make an agreement on how you'll stay connected and how you'll support each other. You could agree to text each other every day and share one thing you're grateful for. It's a fantastic way to stay connected with someone. Your agreement will help you keep each other accountable and motivated.

It's like running. If I sign up to run a half-marathon, I'll need to train for a few months before the event. If I have a running group that shows up at my door at 6 a.m. every morning, I'll be much more likely to stick to my plan than if I'm just running by myself. If I'm by myself, the alarm rings at 5:45 and the truth is that I might just keep hitting snooze until it's time to get up for work. My friends keep me motivated. It makes it more fun. That fun and camaraderie is a positive reinforcement for my good habit and makes it easier to keep it up.

### Gratitude around the dinner table

Go around the table with your family and take turns sharing something you're grateful for, and why. The "and why" is really important. It helps us process in a more tangible way why we feel what we feel.

This is a good one to do with your kids. You can also set the rule that there are no repeats. Meaning, when asked "What are you grateful for today?" the eight-year-old can't just say "recess" every time. They have to go deeper. They have to think of something new.

### The gratitude journal

Happier. Less stress. More optimism. Sounds good, right?

You may have already tried keeping a journal. Maybe you still have it, with three entries from the past four years. To build a better habit, we need a better system.

First, go buy a journal, or ask a loved one to buy one for you. The act of buying it or receiving it will give the journal a special meaning. If you're like me and you hate waste, you won't want to waste your special journal.

Next, put that journal on your pillow where you sleep. When you get in bed to sleep, you'll have to move it. Since you're already moving it, you might as well write something in it, even if it's one thing. Maybe that one thing turns into three things. In the morning, put it back on your pillow.

## Gratitude to start meetings

Many meetings at LinkedIn start with a quick round of gratitude. Sometimes it's a personal or professional win. Sometimes it's a "kudo," a type of gratitude for a teammate. This works best for regular staff meetings, where we know each other. It's a fantastic way to get to know each other as humans first, co-workers next. It also orients the entire team toward optimism. From this place, we're going to be more creative. We're going to be more respectful of each other. We're going to be a better team.

## Gratitude for self

It starts with us. How can we love others if we don't love ourselves? How can we see the good in others if we don't see the good in ourselves? Every day, as you're getting ready, brushing your teeth, putting your makeup on, shaving—stop. Look at yourself in the mirror. Put your hand on your heart. Say, "(Name), I love you." Follow that with one or two things that you appreciate about yourself and why. Something like, "I am organized, and that helps my family thrive." Or, "I am good at staying calm. This helps me come up with better solutions when things are stressful." Combine this with your journaling or your gratitude buddy system to make it even more powerful.

## A Love for All of Life

Without loving ourselves, we have emptiness.

When we love ourselves, we can start to love all of life.

We know that our minds do a fantastic job of pointing out all the bad things in life. It's up to us to balance that out with gratitude. Once we start practicing gratitude, we start orienting toward life differently. We see more possibilities. Instead of seeing everything as good or bad, we start to see things as opportunities for learning. It's all part of the experience. All part of the journey.

We see the beauty in the natural landscape. We can appreciate the way the ants travel in a line, or the way the aspens change color in September. We can delight in the happy noises of children or the way our dog goes berserk *every time* the mail carrier arrives. We start to appreciate life in a way that we were blind to before.

We start to have a zest for life that is unstoppable. Contagious. Our compasses start pointing to a north that wasn't on our map before.

Instead of feeling picked on by life, we open up to see our partnership with the Universe.

We start to operate like life is happening *for us* instead of *to us*.

We are glowing. Others recognize the light within us.

We are alive.

## PART III

# The Inner Journey: The Mastery of Me

Yesterday I was clever, so
I wanted to change the world.
Today I am wise, so I am
changing myself.

RUMI

# 10

# CLIMBING THE RIGHT MOUNTAIN (IT'S YOUR CHOICE)

"SHUTE, YOU WANT me to keep your score?"

I'm playing golf with my friend Danny and it's the end of the first hole. I laugh, then say, "Sure. But you know I have a different scoring system, right?"

He looks up, remembering, and grins. "Oh yeah, smiley faces."

"Yep."

"Okay, well, what color smiley face do you want for the first hole?"

"Hmmm, I'm going with a green smiley face."

"Excellent." He writes something down on his card. He's patient. He's also a much better golfer than I am. Since my son left for college, I haven't been playing much. It goes in streaks. The last time I played with Danny, I hadn't played for over a year. At dinner with our wives he had asked if I liked to play golf.

"I don't play much anymore. I'm not very good." I conceded.

"What does that have to do with liking it?"

The simple wisdom of this resonates deeply. Sure, why *does* being good at it have anything to do with liking it? I have been so conditioned to winning, I've lost track of why we play at all.

In junior high football, if we lost a game, we weren't allowed to talk on the bus ride home. We were supposed to marinate in our failure, let it motivate us for next time. Let it seep into our bones that we were losers and needed to work harder to be winners.

We were thirteen years old!

The lesson could not be any clearer. Losing equals failure. Winning equals fun. Want to have fun? You'd better win.

Where was the joy of the sport? The joy of being outside, of being together, building camaraderie?

Just win, *then* you can think of those things.

Our other two playing partners, friends of Danny's, heard our exchange.

"Wait, what? How does your scoring system work?"

"Easy. I don't play enough to be as good as I want, so expecting every shot to be like it used to be is just going to frustrate me. We're supposed to be having fun out here. I still want to compete, so... the winner is whoever has the most fun. It's like those airport survey machines that ask you about your experience with three or four buttons. Red frowny face. Yellow neutral. Green smiley face."

Peter smiles and chuckles. "Cool."

John smiles, but it seems more like a smirk. I can feel him judging me. Maybe he thinks I'm weak. Not a *real* winner. Somehow not a real man. Or maybe that's all just in my head and John is thinking he's not quite ready for this scoring system. Either way, I decide I don't care.

On the next drive, I hit a beautiful shot.

Peter says, "Green smiley face?"

"Oh yeah. *Definitely* green smiley face." Now that I've declared what winning looks like, I'm committed.

A few holes later I hit a terrible shot, straight off to the side, deep into the brush, never to be seen again. It's like I've never played before. Ugh.

Peter searches my face for a reaction and chuckles. "Red frowny face?"

"No, no, no. Not yet!" I shout, laughing. "No way man! That's not how this works." I drop another ball and hit again, trying to remind myself why I'm here. Yes, of course, part of me wants to toss my club and pout. Isn't that what we're supposed to do? If we lose, we're not supposed to show any happiness at all. We're supposed to think about that failure all the way home. That was a terrible shot! I know I could have done better. I *wanted* to do better.

At the start of the round, I had introduced myself as the head of mindfulness and compassion programs at LinkedIn. I am something new in their lives. A novelty. They are watching to see what I am all about, what reactions I will have. Now is not a time to throw a tantrum.

*Am I ready for this?* I'm not sure if I can score a green smiley face *no matter what*. I mean, that is the goal, but, it's hard! Really hard. Now I feel pressure. An *expectation* to be happy. It is a game within a game.

I roll my eyes at myself. I will need to let *that* game go as well and *just be*. But... for today, I am focused on winning at green smiley faces.

Danny and Peter have joined in the smiley face discussion for their own shots.

Peter hits a clunker into the rough. I raise my eyebrows and look into his eyes.

"Green smiley face?"

His frustration softens. He laughs. "Ugh! I'm trying! It's so hard. It's harder than golf!" He is smiling. It's working.

"Yeah, that's for sure."

John is not having a great golf day. He also has no interest in our playful banter. He prefers the regular scoring system. He has sunk deeper into himself. With every bad shot his mood sours. He curses more. His jaw tightens. His game declines with his mood as he marinates in the failures. It is an ugly downward spiral.

We stand farther away from him. Keep our light conversation to ourselves. He is holding a long metal club. For my own safety, I do not ask him about smiley faces.

Peter, on the other hand, is catching the spirit. He is the weakest golfer of the four of us, but something about the new scoring system is resonating with him. With another terrible shot he shouts, "Oh yeah! Dang it. Another chance to freaking practice!" There is lightness, joy in his eyes.

He smiles, shakes his head, and sighs, reaching for another ball. Hole by hole, his mood improves, regardless of his game. As his mood gets better, he relaxes a bit, and his golf gets better as well.

Over eighteen holes I score sixteen green smileys and two yellow neutrals. Both of the yellow faces were from times when I cursed under my breath after some particularly bad shots. Both times I quickly got back to smiles, and the others didn't hear, but still... I have room for improvement.

At the eighteenth hole, we remove our hats, shake hands, and thank each other for the round. Peter is all smiles. John walks off in a silent rage. He doesn't want to talk. It's time for him to drive home and soak in his failures. To think about being a winner next time.

Red frowny face sucks.

## Border Guards

"How long are you in the country?"

I'm passing through Irish immigration on my way to visit my team in the Dublin office. It's five o'clock in the morning. I have been awake for twenty-six hours. The border guard has just started his shift. He looks at me, looks at my passport picture, and looks back at me with the eyes of someone who would rather be somewhere else.

He is on the verge of a very long sigh.

As an operations guy, I wonder what they call these discussions. Interactions? Tickets? Entrances? Checks?

I wonder how many of these interactions he has had. I'm bored, so I do the math. At one minute each for an eight-hour shift, that's nearly five hundred per day. Two hundred and forty working days a year makes a hundred and twenty thousand(ish) per year. I wonder if he's gotten to a million yet in his career. My instincts say yes. Maybe there's a plaque on a wall somewhere in the back with his picture next to a "million checks" badge.

I don't think so.

"Mr. Shut?" He's staring at his screen.

"Oh, yep, it's Shute, like 'shoot.'" I smile and make a small pretend gun with my finger and thumb, which I waggle in the air, careful not to point at him. He looks up, winces nearly imperceptibly, stifles his very long sigh, and continues.

"Mr. Shute, how long are you in the country?" He returns his gaze back to his screen.

"Umm, let's see, what day is today? Tuesday? I'm here through Friday." It's early. I've just gotten off a twelve-hour flight. I'm not so clear about time.

"Nature of your visit?"

"I'm here on business." I'm thinking about making a really terrible dad joke about nature, wishing I was outdoors, but even at five in the morning I have the sense to keep it to myself. I see his stern face and don't want to end up getting detained or body searched.

"And what kind of work do you do?" The next box on his form. I wonder which number I am for him. I'm guessing somewhere between 1.4 and 1.5 million.

"I lead customer service for LinkedIn." I decide to play it straight.

"Lincoln?" Our accents are confusing for each other.

"It's LinkedIn. Like to *link*, to connect." I have more to say but am committing to efficiency.

"What do they do?" He looks into my eyes. I search his face for meaning. Is he testing me, deciding if I really work at LinkedIn? Has he genuinely never heard of LinkedIn? We have over six hundred million members. I guess he isn't one of them.

I continue playing it straight.

"It's a social networking site for professionals."

He makes the "and?" look with his eyes. The rest of his face is stone. I continue, trying to find the right words in the shortest phrasing.

"We help people find jobs. We help them stay connected to their colleagues. We help people stay informed. We help make them better at their jobs." I'm a bit proud of myself for remembering and articulating some of our core value propositions so cleanly at five in the morning.

He looks up, stone-faced. "Can they help me be better at my job?" He isn't looking for a response. I shrug the shrug that silently says, *I don't know, maybe?*

He can't control his long sigh anymore. He stares at nothing on his desk for a few beats. Then he hands me back my passport and slowly finds my eyes again.

"I work for the state." He pauses. I have to go very far inside to read his eyes. "Have a nice stay," he says crisply, without emotion.

He looks toward the line of disoriented travelers and raises his voice.

"Next."

A FEW months later, my friend Lana also arrives at Irish immigration. She has had a very long and unexpected layover in Newark. She doesn't sleep well on planes. Actually, she doesn't sleep at all. She has tried all the tricks. Adjust to the new time as soon as you're on the plane. No alcohol or caffeine. Drink as much water as you can. Take a melatonin when it's time to sleep.

Still, here she is in line at immigration, bleary-eyed, dazed. For two minutes in line, she can't find her passport. Purse, backpack, back to purse, from pocket to pocket, panic starting to rise in her throat. Then, there it is, right where she had looked before. She mutters to herself. Thinks about her pillow at home. She just wants to sleep.

"Next," says the border guard.

She approaches and hands him her passport and customs form.

"Good morning! How are ya?" he says. His eyes are clear.

"Oh, I'm okay. That was a long flight." She still wants to sleep.

"Ah, I'm sorry about that. Well, at least it's another *lovely* sunny day in Dublin," he says with great enthusiasm. Lana looks outside in the twilight. It's foggy. Maybe even raining. Cold. She looks back at him and smiles. Perks up a bit.

"And what brings you to Ireland?" He is much more awake than she is.

"Well, I'm a writer. I'm here to visit a friend and help tell her story."

"A writer! Well, you've come to the right place. Can't move about a pub without trippin' over a poet. This is the land of the silver tongues." He exaggerates his accent for the last part. Gives her a little wink.

"So, what's the story?" He stops what he is doing and searches her eyes for the glimmer. She pauses, searches his face in return to see if he is really interested.

He is.

She smiles. Her eyes sparkle. "Well, it's a *good* one. My friend, who is in her forties, has fallen in love for the first time."

The border guard cocks his head, waiting for more. His eyes are alive.

"The problem is, she's just gotten engaged—and not to the person she fell in love with."

"Intriguing," nods the guard. Lana continues.

"The problem is, she's fallen in love with a woman." The border guard's face lights up. A wide smile sneaks across it. His eyebrows are up.

"My friend is Indian, from a very traditional Hindu family." Lana has been stringing the story along, letting it build. Now she's fully awake. She's doing what she does best. She's a story-teller and she's found an audience.

"Oh my God!" Exclaims the border guard, loud enough for the guard behind him to look up sharply. She waits a few beats for dramatic effect. Now it's time to deliver the goods. She's glowing.

"And... the woman she's fallen in love with is Muslim."

"Nooooo!" He says, standing up from his chair. His mouth is open in genuine disbelief and wonder. "You can't make that up. It's too good!" He sits back down, considering what he's just heard, shaking his head. "Brilliant. Genius. Just brilliant. Now *that's* a story that needs writing. You've come to the right place. Add a little Irish magic..." His voice trails off. He's lost in the story.

The guard's smile is in full bloom. Lana is in full bloom as well, freshly excited to see her friend. Excited to be here, in the land of poets. The land of possibility, of hidden magic.

Leprechauns. She hasn't considered that before. Now she sees herself as part of a bigger whole, connected to a long line of storytellers. James Joyce. Samuel Beckett. Oscar Wilde. Jonathan Swift. And now, Lana. It's perfect.

Poetic.

She is ready.

"Have a wonderful time in Ireland. I hope to read your story someday." The guard smiles again.

"Why, thank you. Have a great day." She takes in his smile as she walks away.

"Next," he says, his voice even more chipper than before.

Lana floats away, glowing. The air crackles with possibility.

## Choice

I'm sitting in a meeting that I don't want to be in. We're doing a quarterly review for a part of the business that I'm not very involved in. The presenting team has put a ton of work into this. Late nights for the past few days to get ready. Dealing with the stress and anxiety of presenting to the executive team. It's their baby. It's their chance to make their mark.

For me, it's of mild interest. I'm not part of the exec team or the presenting team. The rest of us—fifty to sixty people across several rooms—are here in case we're needed. We're here to stay informed. We're here to show face. I can feel the pull of work back at my desk. I have my own projects that are calling me. I need to get stuff done. Otherwise, it will be me who's working late at night to catch up. But I'm here. I'm expected to be here. Or at least, that's the story I'm telling myself. I *feel* like I'm expected to be here. Every fiber in my being wants to leave, wants to go back to my desk and do my own thing. Being here makes me feel trapped. Makes me frustrated. Makes me unsatisfied.

There's a tax to being part of a team, part of something bigger than ourselves. It's the tax of being in meetings that don't have much to do with us. It's the tax of attending your niece's eighth grade graduation. It's the tax of standing in line at Disneyland while waiting your turn to ride Pirates of the Caribbean.

That tax is doing anything we don't really want to do, and being required to do it because we're part of something bigger. We start to feel like we're trapped. It's something we *have* to do. We feel like a victim.

The truth is, we have a choice.

In nearly every situation we have a choice.

We could leave that meeting. We could skip our niece's graduation. We don't *have* to go to Disneyland.

We might say to ourselves, "Oh, that's not true. I can't skip the meeting. My manager expects me there." "I can't skip my niece's graduation. My brother's family came to *my* daughter's graduation." "I can't skip Disneyland. My kids are excited about it."

All true. There's a consequence for each of our choices.

We don't *have* to do anything we don't want to at work. We could quit our jobs. We don't *have* to do anything we don't want to with our families. We could leave our relationships.

We're choosing. We're *choosing* to stay in the meeting. We're *choosing* to go to Anisha's graduation. We're *choosing* to stand in line. Or not.

For some choices, the consequences are severe. Leaving our relationships, leaving a job—those are serious life choices that should not be taken lightly. There's something powerful about contrasting our choices so severely. It makes it easier to decide to choose to stay.

When we shift from *having* to do something to *choosing* to do something, the frustration and anxiety start to fall away. Sometimes this is extraordinarily hard. Leaving a relationship, when there is history, and families, and kids involved.

Leaving a job when finances are tough, and you don't know where you'll find work next. We can feel trapped. We can feel like extras in our own movie.

Regardless of what we choose, the act of choosing sets us free. It's hard to feel like a victim when we're the ones calling the shots. In each moment we can take the attitude "I chose this. I'm choosing to be here. Now I'm going to make the best of it."

Back to my quarterly business review. I realize I'm not needed by the team presenting. I can read the notes later if I really need to know what happens. I realize that I'm there because of my own internal pressure to show face, not to actively provide value.

I pack up my laptop and my notebook and make my way to the door. There's no need to slink. I don't need to feel ashamed or guilty. In this case, I'll add more value to this group, to this company, by getting my own work done. Next time, it might work out the other way. Even though it's not my area, maybe I have value to add and I choose to stay in the meeting.

I am not a victim of inertia.

I have chosen.


## Laird

"Who do you most admire?"

A few years ago, I was taking a workshop on values. The instructor asked us to identify three people, living or dead, that we most admired. Once we had selected our three, we went on to detail the qualities about them that we most appreciated.

I chose Abraham Lincoln, for his wisdom, courage, and insights into human behavior. Without him the fate of America would be uncertain.

I chose Gandhi, for his wisdom, courage, and determination. Without him the fate of India would be uncertain.

I chose my friend Laird, for his wisdom, for the way he parents, for the way he is. Without him and people like him, the fate of the human race would be uncertain.

Laird is my neighbor. I get to see Laird in action. He and his wife, Sharon, have five children, all girls. When you have five kids in the house, there's always some form of chaos. There's always drama. I'm the youngest of five. I can relate.

Laird navigates this drama with the patience of stone. He speaks to his girls in reverent tones. He is calm like a mirrored pool of clear water on a moonlit night. I've never heard him raise his voice. He is there for them. He is fully present. If there's a gathering of adults and Laird is in the middle of a conversation and one of the girls arrives with a problem, Laird handles it with grace. He does not dismiss their needs. He does not shoo them away. He acknowledges them. He values them. He loves them. They are his sun and moon and stars.

If you ask him about his job, he will first tell you his job is to be there for Sharon and the girls. They are his number one priority. He is a model for how to live as love itself. You don't need to go to a monastery or a church to find it. Just watch Laird parent.

Laird is not a CEO. He is not a wealthy man. He didn't go to business school. He didn't go to college. Laird is a small business owner—he has a couple of trucks and a couple of men who work for him. They clean carpets. They do some light janitorial work. It is not glamorous in any way. There are no public accolades. No press. No social media praise. It is solitary, silent, quiet work.

Laird has chosen this work. He has chosen it for the flexibility it provides him to be present as a father and a husband. He could grow his business. He could buy more trucks, hire more men. That would mean more time away. He chooses to scale his business in a way that values time with family over money.

Sometimes when Laird is out on a job, he and the client will get to talking. Because of the way Laird is, because of the depth and clarity in his eyes, the client feels safe. They just might find their way into a conversation about life, about their own problems. They will feel compelled to share with Laird. He will listen. He will be present. He might offer a nugget of patient wisdom. For the client, it will seem like a miracle, like Laird was sent to them by the Universe at the right place, the right time. A calm pond in the hurricane of their life.

Laird is not perfect. He has his own problems. He has his own trauma that needs to be healed. But if you need a friend, if you need a father, if you need to be heard, to know that you are not alone, Laird will be there.

Financially, Laird might live on the edge of chaos.

But he lives with a deep faith that he is loved. That his primary job in life is to love.

He's the richest man I know.

## We're in Charge

In every moment we have a choice.

When we see the cages that have been built around us, that we have built ourselves, our illusions fade away and we are left with responsibility. We become like the dog that carries its own leash.

We're in charge.

We can define success for ourselves.

We can choose how we'll keep score.

We can choose how we think about our work, our duties.

We can choose how we respond to life.

In this choice lies our freedom.

What are you choosing?

Where does poetry live?
In the eye that says, "Wow wee,"
From the heart saying, shouting,
"I am so damn alive!"

**HAFIZ**

# 11

# THE REFRAME

THE SKY HAS turned green and is churning as if it's in a giant mixing bowl and being stirred. I've never seen clouds act like this before. I'm ten years old and watching the storm unfold from behind our giant kitchen window on the farm.

The wind is coming from every direction at once. Leaves and tumbleweeds and anything not bolted down is being blown around. The flag near our driveway is at full attention, straining at the gale. We're watching TV, getting live updates. The local news station confirms what we see out the window: we're in a severe weather warning. High winds, heavy rain, possible tornado activity. And hail. The radar map shows a bright red blob, menacing directly toward us.

We're scanning the sky, watching for tendrils of clouds spinning. An eerie feeling seeps into the kitchen like an intruder. There's nothing we can do to stop it.

From our porch it's eight running steps to the root cellar. It's essentially an underground bunker that creates a dirt hump in the earth. A door lays tilted on the ground, the entrance to the cavern below. Ancient and roughly formed cement steps lead down into the dark. It's cool and damp down there. And usually kinda gross. Shelves against the wall hold the bounty of previous garden activity. Glass mason jars hold green beans, tomatoes, pickles, and jam. Sometimes there are little garter snakes that squirm around. Or a toad, happy to find a cool, dark hiding spot in the heat of July. It's dark. There are no lights.

A few years before, we had retreated to the cellar when the sky erupted in wild clouds, funnels darting in and out in every direction, even upward. None of them became full tornadoes on the ground near us, but thirty miles away there was chaos.

I look at the cellar door from the kitchen and scrunch my nose. I don't want to go there unless we have to.

From the window I can see water gushing down our gravel driveway. The rain is so dense we can no longer see the flagpole fifty feet away. As the rain eases, it is replaced with heavy, single, distinct drops, pinging the tin-roofed garage. Pinging the metal downspouts and rain gutters.

And then the hail begins.

At first it's the size of a pea. It bounces off the grass and gives the illusion that it's coming from the ground, popcorn leaping up eight inches. It's exciting. Mesmerizing. The patter and pinging then turns into scary thumping as the hail grows. Now it is less regular, less frequent, more concentrated and severe, like a boxer moving from quick bursts of jabs, then throwing back his shoulder and delivering a heavy uppercut. Chunks the size of golf balls now smash the gravel driveway. The tin roofs on the outer buildings become a symphony of drums erupting in a cacophony of destruction.

I am outside on the covered porch, spellbound. The air is electric. I have grabbed my heavy plastic costume football helmet. I am planning on running out and grabbing some of those giant hailstones. I want to see them for myself. Against my mother's better judgment, I rush out with a small plastic bucket to collect the biggest ones. I race back to the porch, darting and diving, thinking if I'm nimble enough I can avoid the falling stones. They are amazing. The smaller pieces of hail have frozen together to form larger chunks, nearly the size of my fist, like ice cubes stuck together in the freezer. It's hard to believe these things have fallen from the sky.

As things settle down and the weather clears, my sister and I inspect our icy treasures. We put them in the freezer and will eventually pull them out to show any sibling or neighbor who had missed the show. I am giddy with excitement.

My father is less excited. He's still standing on the porch, leaning against a railing, long after the show is over and the rest of us have retreated inside. He isn't ready to come in. My mother goes to stand next to him. He has that look of someone in deep introspection after a funeral service.

Heavy.

As a ten-year-old, I have no appreciation for what has just happened. For me, it's a bit of meteorological theater. It's the most exciting thing that has happened over the whole summer. For my dad, it's the destruction of his plans. The hail has destroyed the wheat, which was over half of our income for the year. The expenses are still there. The planting, the fertilizer, the care and attention and labor of nearly a full year. That has already happened. And here, a few weeks before the harvest, after a year's worth of work, in twenty minutes it is all gone.

Farming was already problematic. The oil embargo of the late 1970s had caused fuel and fertilizer prices to skyrocket, but somehow the price of grain for farmers remained low. The year before, the combine harvester had caught fire during the wheat harvest. My dad escaped, unharmed but rattled. The very expensive combine, and the field of wheat around it, were destroyed. They were not insured. We needed that harvest to catch back up. To catch our breath. To catch a break.

The red blob on the radar screen starts meandering past us. It is still giant, larger than the area of the farm. Every field of wheat has been smothered by this dark red blob.

This is bad.

Over the next day or two, my dad grows quieter, but I never see him lose hope. He is resilient. He does not complain. He'll smile, shake his head, and say, "We'll figure it out. We always have."

Forward. Always forward.

This was how it was for my father. No matter what happened. No matter which hand of cards life dealt him year after year, he persisted. For nearly sixty years he farmed, a calm gambler at the high stakes table with low stakes in his pocket. He kept at it, his stack of chips rising and falling with the weather and the markets. He could control only what he could control. He knew there would be ups and downs. The down, he shrugged off. Got back to work.

He loved farming. It was in his bones. He was exactly where he wanted to be, living the life he had imagined.

He created his own port in the storm. He also knew where his real wealth lived. He had a loving partner. Five healthy and thriving kids. Community. He had everything he needed.

He made it so.

Always moving forward.

"We'll figure it out. We always have."

## Karaoke

"How are you feeling?"

We usually don't spend much time *really* thinking about the answer to this question. Imagine you're about to go onstage and sing karaoke in front of strangers. You've picked out a song that you sort of know, you've got the mic in your hand.

"How are you feeling?"

Maybe you've got butterflies in your stomach. Maybe you're living in the future, thinking about standing onstage and wondering if you'll forget the words. Maybe you're imagining looking out and having hundreds of eyes on you and feeling embarrassed.

Or maybe you're living in the future, excited about what could happen. You're thinking about the high fives and admiration as you come offstage. You're thinking about enjoying the performance.

Alison Brooks, a researcher at Harvard, did an experiment that was later published in the *Journal of Experimental Psychology*.[6] She was working with people who were about to sing karaoke.

The first group was told to respond "I'm feeling anxious" when asked about how they were feeling. Then they went and sang their song.

The second group was instructed to say "I'm feeling excited." Then they proceeded to sing their song.

She was using Nintendo Wii's *Karaoke Revolution: Glee*. It gave an objective measure of their performance. It essentially measures accuracy of pace and pitch.

What do you think happened?

The "I'm feeling anxious" group had accuracy scores in the 50s. The "I'm feeling excited" participants had accuracy scores in the 80s.

The stories we tell ourselves about how we're feeling are powerful. The labels we use on ourselves and others are powerful.

A few years ago I started to become aware of some of my blanket responses. If someone asked me how I was doing, I thought of my schedule, packed with work and family and life. I would say, "I'm busy!" The more I said it, the more this label became my brand, my identity, both for me and for others. People would start their sentences, "Hey, I know you're super busy..."

When we tell ourselves and others how incredibly busy we are, you know what life gives us?

More busy.

We're creating our lives all the time with these labels. These thoughts, these perceptions, are powerful. Are we actually that busy? Maybe. All those activities in our lives—the work, the kids' comp soccer, the church board meetings, the social events—we put those there. Each one is a choice that we're making.

What if we acted as if these things in our life were put there on purpose? How would we describe our lives if we were the star of our own movie instead of a victim?

"Scott, how are you doing?"

"Life is great!"

Or, if it's not feeling so great at that moment, maybe...

"Life is full."

Either way, there's a recognition that I have choices. I'm responsible for most of the situations in my life. Even with the ones I'm not responsible for, I'm responsible for how I'm responding to the situation.

This reframing to optimism isn't just a feel-good strategy (it's that too). It gives us better results.

Anxious? Excited?

The first step is to be aware of the story we're telling ourselves and others.

That awareness gives us choice.

That choice leads to freedom.

## We Manifest

Every single thought creates our future.

Our words create our future.

Our attitudes create our future.

Our actions create our future.

When the future happens to us, why do we act so surprised?

## The Lifters

*Boom.*

The windows in the workout room visibly vibrate. The floor shakes.

My immediate reaction is frustration. A flash of anger. I can feel my heart speed up. I'm already breathing, trying to relax.

*Boom.*

The floors and windows shake again.

I'm leading a group meditation at work with eight people on a Thursday afternoon. We're in a larger wood-floored room with mirrors and big windows on one side. It's the same room where all the group exercise classes are held. TRX, HIIT, yoga, boot camp—they're all held here. It's at the back of the gym.

On the way in I had walked past three guys getting ready to do deadlifts together. It's a powerlifting move in which you take a very heavy bar and lift it from the floor, straightening your legs, bringing the bar level to your hips, and then replacing the bar on the ground. Typically, the "replacing the bar on the ground" part means dropping it onto a rubber mat. They had a huge bar prepared, over three hundred pounds. They were getting hyped.

*Boom.*

Every forty-five seconds. The giant crash is followed by yelping and high fiving. I wince. I can feel a rush of frustration rising within. I am trying to just let it be.

I play out a couple of scenarios. In my mind I go to the door, open it, and say, "Hey, hey, hey!" to get their attention. "We're doing a meditation session in here. You guys are shaking the whole frickin' room! Can you do that another time, please?"

My voice would convey my annoyance. I am searching inside for compassion and understanding, but in this scenario, there is no room for that. I just need them to stop. I need them to understand my point of view—clearly *my* practice is more important than theirs.

Um, yeah. That isn't going to work.

I decide it's probably poor form when leading a meditation to stop and scream at people around you who are making noise.

I imagine myself going into a tirade, chewing these guys out, red in the face.

Then I'd come back and continue leading the meditation. Maybe I'd give calming instructions like, "Whatever happens, just let it be part of your experience. Notice, without judgment, what is around you." This strikes me as funny. I let out a little chuckle, smiling.

These weightlifters are having a good time. They are joyful. They are enjoying each other's company. They are probably being fully present—not thinking about work or other stress. In their own way, they are practicing a type of mindfulness.

In this moment I have a choice.

I choose to be joyful.

I decide that each time I hear the boom and feel the shake, I will smile and inwardly say, "Thank you." Thank you for the opportunity to practice my practice. Each boom is a call to action, a sharpening of my senses, a reminder of how far I've come and how much more work I have to do.

Twenty minutes straight.

Every forty-five seconds.

*Boom!*

Smile.

Thank you.

When we finish, the lifters finish at the same time. *Exactly* the same time. I don't believe in coincidence.

During our discussion after the session, we talk about our experience. No one seemed to mind. One guy, a newcomer to our group, says, "Once we got going, I didn't really notice it."

Yes!

This is how life works.

When we're *really* focused, locked in on something positive, the other stuff, the irritations, simply fade from our attention. They're still there. They don't go away. The actual situation doesn't change.

*We* change.

We become more open. We become more centered, more present. More of who we really want to be.

We become our True Self.

## Create Your Life

Every minute of every day we're creating. With our thoughts, our attitudes, our actions. Usually we're asleep at the wheel while we're doing this—just reacting. We can take the wheel and create what we want.

Get quiet for a bit. Take some deep breaths. Let the tension of the day melt away.

Really take a moment.

Breathe.

Settle.

When you're ready, make a declaration of what you want in life.

Say it in present tense.

"I am..."

Here are some ideas. When you're done, make your own list. Write it down. Say it every day. Live it every day. Actively adjust until it is true.

I am a good parent.

I am a loving spouse.
I am generous.
I am compassionate.
I love myself unconditionally.
I love others unconditionally.
I am brave.
I am successful at what I do.
I am...

## Happiness

Viktor Frankl wrote the book *Man's Search for Meaning*. He had the experience of being imprisoned in a Nazi concentration camp during World War II. Here's what he has to say.

> When we are no longer able to change a situation, we are challenged to change ourselves.
>
> Everything can be taken from a man but one thing: the last of the human freedoms—to choose one's attitude in any given set of circumstances, to choose one's own way.
>
> Between stimulus and response there is a space. In that space is our power to choose our response. In our response lies our growth and our freedom.[7]

Given his experiences, you might expect him to be focused on his suffering. On his pain. He's not talking about being in prison. He's talking about freedom.

Happiness.

Life happens. It's up to us to decide how we'll respond to it. Our happiness is based on that response, more so than on the events in our lives. We see the extremes. There are miserable billionaires. There are people living in shocking poverty who are content and happy. The opposite is true as well.

Life happens.
It's up to us to decide
how we'll respond to it.
Our happiness is based
on that response.

There was a classic study in 1978 by a trio of researchers from Northwestern University and the University of Massachusetts. They followed two groups of people. One group had become wealthy—they won the lottery. The other group had become quadriplegic—they lost the use of their arms and legs. We might assume the lottery winners became happier. We might assume that the people who became quadriplegic became less happy. In the short term, that was true. But over time, people returned to the level of happiness that they experienced before their event. If they started out as a 2 out of 5 on the happiness scale, then a year or two later, regardless of events, they went back to being a 2. If they started out as a 4, they went back to being a 4.[8]

In our own lives, if we have a day where we get promoted, we're most likely going to be much happier than the day we find out our job has been eliminated. But over time, our happiness will settle into what some psychologists call set points. Over the long term, our happiness is governed by these set points. The way to change these set points is to do the inner work.

This reframing of life, this move to optimism, doesn't mean we're sugarcoating things. It doesn't mean we're saying that everything in life is great. That's not mindfulness either. Mindfulness is being aware of the entire situation, without judgment. That awareness gives us choice.

In 1961, President John F. Kennedy was taking a tour of the NASA facilities for the first time. He came across a janitor who was mopping the floor and asked him what he did at NASA. The janitor said he was helping to put a man on the moon. The man was proud, beaming.

Every situation, every challenge in life is an opportunity to test our capability for joy, our capability to connect with something bigger. Every thought, word, and action is a step toward the person we are becoming.

If we choose pessimism, our options are limited. If we choose optimism, the range of possibilities expands greatly.

We can't control the cards that life deals us.

We *can* control how we play them.

It's powerful to shift our perspective from "life is happening *to* me" to "life is happening *for* me." Even if your view on how the world works doesn't align with that thinking, consider it this way: "How would I respond if I had *chosen* this situation to make me stronger?"

We can move from victim to player, to being the star in our own movie.

Sit, be still, and listen.
If light is in your heart, you will
find your way home.

**RUMI**

# 12

# THE FULL BODY YES

HAVE A TOUGH decision to make. My top lieutenant is taking another role and I need to replace him. I am hiring for the most strategic role on my team. This senior director's success will be my success. It feels like everyone is watching. It feels like the biggest hire of my life.

There are two finalists. We have gone through many rounds of interviews. Much feedback and discussion. The interview team, made up of my direct reports and some important cross-functional partners, is split fifty-fifty. We have gotten many people involved because we want them to be part of the change management process. We want them to be part of the decision, so they'll buy in more deeply to whomever we choose.

This is an opinionated bunch.

Half of the team wants the external candidate, Anka. They thinks she's great. They are not convinced the other candidate can do the job.

Half of the team wants the internal candidate, McKensie. They think she's great. They are not convinced the other candidate can do the job.

I have that uncomfortable, boxed-in feeling. I know that no matter which one I choose; I am going to upset half the team. With my life strategy of "likeability," I prefer consensus, or at least majority. It saves me from that ugly conflict. Keeps me safe. This is going to be my decision only. There is no hiding.

I mull it over for a few days. I have my pros and cons list for both candidates. I consider the counsel of everyone involved. It is even. Both are fully capable. We have found the right candidates. There is no more available information to make the call. Either would be okay, but which one is *right*? No amount of further discussion or interviewing will allow me to see into the future, to see how they will lead, how they will vibe with the team, how their true colors fly.

It's decision time. I want to get it right. The stakes are high. In these situations, some people go with their gut. I have something similar in mind, but with a twist.

My mind feels very noisy.

I need to get quiet.

In contemplation, I ask for guidance. I have a conversation with the Universe.

"*Okay*, I don't do this very often, but I need some help here. I need a sign." I take some deep breaths and settle in.

"If it's Anka..." I lightly bring Anka to mind. She is an Indian woman with deep black hair.

"I'll see dark black hair with a bun in the back and a butterfly pin holding it together." I know, it's random. It's the image that came to me.

"And if it's McKensie..." I bring McKensie to mind. I remember that she has a distinctive, bright-orange work bag that she carries around.

"I'll see an orange... rhinoceros." I chuckle to myself. "An orange rhino? How's *that* going to happen?"

I know from trying this technique previously that I need to be specific. I need to pick things that I normally wouldn't encounter. If I choose a silver Prius versus a blue bird, I'll see hundreds of them. I guess I could say, "Okay, whichever I see first, silver Prius or blue bird." Maybe that would make it easier for the Universe.

I want to be sure. I want the secret handshake, the knowing wink, the unmistakable connection.

I finish my contemplation with great gratitude. "Okay, within the next twenty-four hours. Let's go!"

I am convinced that either of the candidates would be fantastic. It will be fine either way. I turn it over to the Universe and put my pros and cons list away. I feel a weight lift from my shoulders.

The next day comes and goes and nothing happens. I kind of forget about my request.

The day after, a Friday, my team and I take off early to watch the Star Wars movie that's opening that day. We're hanging out, enjoying our popcorn, settling in to watch the previews. I'm relaxing, letting the stress of the week start to slip away. I'm in a whispered conversation with my seatmate when I see the screen and freeze.

In the preview for an animated movie, an orange rhinoceros has just rambled across the screen.

My first inclination is, "Wait! Was that orange or red? Kinda red-orange?" I laugh to myself again. Then I have that familiar feeling. The Full Body Yes. It feels right. My mind settles. My body settles. I *know* it is going to work out.

That's it. The decision is made.

I feel connected. Supported.

Loved.

And, of course, McKensie is absolutely fantastic in her new role.

Life is always trying

to tell us something, to

guide us, to teach us.

## You'd Better Listen

When I was a teenager, I was reading the stories of spiritual masters. Their lives seemed so difficult. The trials that they went through on their way to freedom sounded terrible. Some of them lost everything. I wondered, "Why does it have to be so hard?"

One day, I have a conversation with the Universe.

"Hey, if there's a way to do this without all the pain, I'd like to go that route. Can I learn by humor and joy instead?" I am sincere. And scared. I am looking for the easy way.

"Learn to listen," the Universe responds simply.

It isn't a threat. It is simply the answer to my request. Plain and simple. Good advice.

I think life is always trying to tell us something, to guide us, to teach us. We're sitting on our couch in our apartment, and life taps on the door. We think to ourselves, "Was that a tap?" and go back to what we were doing. Then there's a firm knock on the door. We're busy watching our favorite show. We try to ignore it. Then there's a pounding, a kicking of the door. Now we're annoyed. Our favorite show is coming to a *really* exciting part. We can't possibly look away. Then the door gets kicked in. The winds of life rearrange our room. Our furniture is moved. Our stuff is blown out of place. Our life is a mess. Everything changes, whether we like it or not.

We sit in the middle of the chaos, observing the painful rearranging of our lives. Now we're mad at life. We feel victimized. We say, "Hey! Come on! Why didn't you just knock?"

## Detach

I'm coming home from Sunday service with my kids. The weight of the week has lifted a bit. There's been a lot going on. All week I've felt like a tightrope walker, trying to hold a delicate balance while getting blown by the wind. My life is full. In this moment, after service, it feels like the wind has died down. The tightrope has turned into a sidewalk. I can breathe. I feel a bit more free.

My mind has been heavy with a situation going on at work. It's an ongoing problem, one that I don't have control over. I don't know what else I can do. I've been churning and churning on it for a month. It is consuming me.

We're in the car, waiting at a stoplight. Across the intersection I see a giant billboard. It says "Detach."

I snicker out loud, amused. The Universe is very efficient.

"Okay, okay," I say inwardly. "Detach." I take a big breath and exhale. "Got it." I let go. I can feel the letting go in my body. I can feel the settling. The challenge loses its hold on me when I stop holding on to it so tight. I am grateful for the message. The connection.

As I let go, a solution to the challenge becomes apparent. It is one that I had considered before, along with the noise of twenty others. Now it is the clear favorite. An obvious next step. I smile and shake my head at my struggle. I smile at the ease I now feel.

As we pull through the intersection, I can see the sign fully. Part of it had been obstructed by trees from my previous vantage point. It is an ad for a new housing development in Morgan Hill. It says "Detached Homes from the $600s."

## The Kam Show

"I need your help."

I'm in a meeting on a Monday afternoon. My pocket buzzes. I see I've a missed call from my son, Kameron. The meeting will be over in twenty minutes. I'll try to call him then. My phone buzzes again. It's Kam.

The meeting I'm in is a biannual review. The team presenting has been preparing for days to give me an update. For a couple of them, it's their one shot this year to share what they're doing. Their one shot this year to get face time with me and the leadership team. Some of them feel like the weight of their career rests on this meeting.

I text Kam. "Can I call you in 20. In a mtg."

I look back up. I feel guilty for not paying attention. I also feel guilty for not leaving the meeting immediately to call him. I'm torn between work and family. I'm torn between my commitments. It's not the first time.

Kam texts back. "Please call me now. I need your help."

I excuse myself and step into the hallway to call him. He answers, upset.

"Dad, it's bad. The paint spilled everywhere."

The day before we had been cleaning out the garage. There was a stack of old half-filled paint cans. Some of them had dried up. Others were obsolete—colors that had been painted over long ago. We found a paint store that recycles old paint and loaded up the pickup. I was glad to be rid of the cans. But when we got to the store, we found out they were closed on Sundays.

Kam has just turned sixteen. Has just gotten his driver's license. He has only driven solo a few times. I thought it would be a good adventure for him to return the cans without me. He is learning self-reliance and independence. The paint store is in a part of town we don't visit much. On the way home he had tried to memorize the route, paying attention to the street signs and landmarks. I was thinking about my own dad and each increasingly challenging task I had been given at the same age on the farm. I had smiled at the connection.

When I had left this morning, I reminded Kam about the cans. His response was less than enthusiastic. He didn't quite view it with the same level of adventure or excitement.

Now, on the phone, Kam is really upset. Scared. Frustrated.

"People drive so crazy. This guy pulled right in front of me. I slammed on the brakes. When I did that, the paint cans smashed to the front, and when they did, they spilled." I'm having a hard time understanding what he's saying. He's nearly in tears and speaking as fast as he can.

"People are screaming at me," he says.

"What do you mean, people are screaming at you?"

"I kept driving, then this guy is behind me, honking. He pulls up beside me at a light and is screaming at me 'cause the paint is dripping down the back of the truck. He's scream- ing something about the environment, how I'm killing the environment—I don't know. I don't know what to do! There's paint everywhere! It's on the truck. What do I do?"

"Woah," I say, taking it all in. This is bad. I don't really know what to do, either. I'm trying to focus fully on him. I'm feeling a bit helpless. I'm thinking about the meeting that I left. We can reschedule. They'll understand. It's not great. Some of the team has traveled to the Bay Area just for this meeting. I feel bad for them. But I know they'll understand.

And even if I leave right now, with traffic I'm still forty min- utes away from Kam.

Kam is telling other parts of the story. It's a jumble of con- fusion and frustration. He is at his limit. I wish I could be there. I wish I could make his pain go away.

"Okay, just breathe for a second. Take a big..."

"No, no, I can't. I'm freaking out."

I'm trying to maintain my own composure, to tamp down my own stress so I can be there for him.

"I know, I know, just slow down a bit. Just... slow... down."

"That's easy for you to say! You're in your nice office. I'm out here with people screaming at me." He's got a point. It's a lot easier to think of what we're supposed to do when it's not happening to us.

"I need your help. Please come home."

I hear the desperation in his voice. I return to my meeting, apologizing. We agree to reschedule and wrap things up. I ask my assistant to move the rest of the day's meetings. I quickly grab my things and head to the car.

This choice seems obvious, but it's still not easy for me. I am torn, deeply feeling the responsibilities I have at work. People are counting on me, looking up to me. I was raised with the values of "do what you say you're going to do" and "duty."

The internal tension gives me a knot in my stomach.

Kam has been gaining independence. It is important that he have some experiences to figure things out by himself. But this one is complicated. I'm not even sure what to do about the paint. My instincts are to help and protect him. I want to be there with him.

The panic and need in his voice make it easier to choose— to leave work.

I've been in the car for ten minutes when Kam calls again. I'm in bumper-to-bumper traffic. Trapped. I'll be there in thirty minutes. This time he's swearing. He has taken the truck to a do-it-yourself car wash.

"I was washing the truck and the guy who runs the car wash saw me and told me I had to leave. That I couldn't wash the paint out there. Dad, there's paint *everywhere*! I can't get it off the truck!" There is anger and frustration in his voice. Much of it is directed at me.

"Why didn't *you* just do. this?" he nearly shouts. I had given him the task. It was turning out to be way harder than I expected.

"Where are you?" he asks. I tell him I am still stuck in traffic and that I'll be another thirty minutes at least. He mutters a few ugly words and hangs up.

I feel it all. The strain and tension of leaving work, leaving my obligations, my responsibilities. The heat from our conversation. I am reacting to his anger. Mostly I feel for Kam. I want to be there. I had given him this task and now it is blowing up. I want to fix it. To make it better.

Now!

Instead, I am stuck in the car, not moving fast enough. I feel the crunch of time. Both my body and my mind are racing. The cars in front of me are all irritating me. I want to shout—*get out of the way!* I imagine the future of flying cars and fantasize about floating up out of my lane and zipping away.

I stew in silence, trying to calm down, trying to settle. I turn off the music to have some quiet. My mind is providing plenty of noise.

Suddenly I catch sight of the license plate of the car in front of me, and I laugh out loud. I have to look twice. I can't believe it.

The license plate says "KAMSHOW." A wave of calm soothes my body. I relax.

KAMSHOW.

As in, The Kam Show.

A little sign from the Universe. A little "golden-tongued wisdom."

This is Kam's Show. This is his problem to figure out. There is something important about the lesson for him to experience. It is not mine to fix. It is a gift from the Universe to him. It is not my tension to hold. I can let go.

I settle. Everything is going to be *okay*. This is happening for a reason. There is goodness at work here if I can just recognize it. If I can be part of the wave instead of fighting against it. My mind becomes clear. I feel at peace. I turn the music back on, looking for a beat. I drive the rest of the way relaxed. Grateful.

Sometimes, when we're freaking out, when we're overloaded and we have forgotten to slow down and tune in to that deeper part of ourselves, the Universe finds a different way to get a message to us. In this case it was a license plate.

I pull into our driveway right after Kam has. With the help of some great advice from mom, he has found a solution. He's still rattled, but he has done it. The truck isn't perfect. Some small splotches of dull brown paint stay on the bed and tailgate as a reminder for both of us. The wave of challenge has passed.

I can relax.

I am able to listen to his tale, hear him recount his story again. I am able to be clear and loving and supportive.

And not make it about me.

Take a bit of inventory. When have you followed the inner guidance in your life? Trusted your gut? Went with a hunch? Or have you ever gotten it wrong? Heard the information, but didn't act on it? What happened?

We can increase our capacity to listen and trust this information—to calibrate and learn the difference between that True Self talking or the little self, the ego.

Here's the recipe for working with life:

*Be open.* We have enough humility to receive information.

*Trust.* We believe in ourselves. We believe that we can access something deeper. This belief creates a doorway to possibility.

*Take action.* This completes the cycle. The Universe provides a gift. We receive the gift and put that information to use to make our lives and the lives of those around us better.

How do I
Listen to others?
As if everyone were my Master
Speaking to me his
Cherished last words.

**HAFIZ**

# 13

# GETTING TO KNOW BEFORE GETTING TO YES

"I DON'T THINK I'M going to find her here."

It's Saturday night, my sophomore year in college. My friend Alyssa and I are hanging out in my dorm room. We're commiserating about our love lives, or lack of them. My heart has just been broken. I had been trying to manifest a relationship. I had made a Top Ten list of all the things I thought I wanted in a woman. I reviewed it every night. I asked the Universe to send her to me. I knew all would be well in the world when it happened.

It went something like...

The Girlfriend List

- Engineering or science student
- Five-foot-six
- Athletic body
- Wicked sense of humor
- Interested in spiritual teachings
- And more...

Oh, I knew exactly what I wanted. I placed my order to the Universe, took a number, and waited.

I got exactly what I asked for.

It was amazing. Until it wasn't.

It was terrible.

Absolutely.

Freakin'.

Terrible.

And now it is over. I am wallowing in the wreckage of my love life, wondering how my perfect plan, which had been executed perfectly and manifested perfectly, had turned out so very, very imperfectly. Alyssa has no answers. She is also searching for someone. She knows about heartbreak and longing. She has just told me the roller-coastery painful story about her own breakup.

I am frustrated. I left a town where there were about forty girls my age and migrated to the college experience, where there are about ten thousand girls my age. I had assumed the odds were in my favor. Something had told me it was not to be, that I could keep planning and scheming and manifesting, but... well, just don't get your hopes up.

"I just don't think she's here," I moan.

Alyssa smiles, looks up at the sky, and shakes her head. She puts her face in her hands and lets out her own frustrated "Gaaaaahhhhhhhhh! Where are they?"

We sit in contemplative silence for a long time.

"She's probably in India somewhere."

Alyssa raises her eyebrows and scrunches them. She has no comeback.

A few years later, I'm twenty-three. I've just moved to Dallas to start adulting. On top of the excitement of starting a new job, moving to a new state, and building a new life, I have a deep feeling, a knowing, that I am about to meet my life partner, my wife.

I know I am an outlier. Zero of my guy friends are thinking about getting married. Meeting people, dating, hooking up— totally. Marriage ... not so much.

My friends and I are standing just inside the gates of adulthood, the world at our fingertips, finally with some money in our pockets. We have been released from late night homework, tedious labs, and the infinite grind of engineering school. We are free. I keep my knowing to myself.

In Dallas there are too many women my age to count. The math is in my favor. Now it's just a matter of time. I am on high alert.

I have given up making lists of female character traits— things I want. I am learning to work with life at a different level. I don't realize it yet, but I have stumbled into making a list of things that *we* might want.

I have a new list.

The Life Partner List

- Aligned emotionally
- Aligned mentally
- Aligned spiritually
- We make each other happy
- We love and support each other
- Above all: whatever the Universe thinks is best

I figure if I am going to manifest something, I am better off giving more generalities and letting life fill in the blanks.

I am headed to a weekend spiritual seminar in San Diego. I can feel the pull, the magnetism of creation happening out there in the wild of life outside my head. I put it all together. The math is obvious.

I have a *knowing* that I am going to meet my life partner.

I am headed to a retreat of likeminded people.

So ... this must be it. It's time.

*Let's go!*

On the plane I read books of poetry from Rumi, a Persian poet from the thirteenth century. Recently I've been having very live dreams about being a whirling dervish. Spinning under the moon on the desert floor. Tuning in. Rumi's words connect me to this ancient feeling. Memory.

I arrive at the seminar. I've picked up my badge from registration. I sit down at a public bench to thumb through the program and plan out my weekend. I've been there for five minutes.

An absolutely gorgeous woman sits down beside me. She's stunning. She looks like she might be a dancer. She looks like she might be of Persian descent.

I smile.

*Boom!*

The Universe didn't waste any time.

I start a conversation. I don't have much game. With her I don't need to. It flows naturally, like it was meant to be. Like it has been there from the beginning of time. We spend the afternoon together, catching up like old friends. Like we'd been together seven hundred years ago. Two halves of a magnet, snapping together after a lengthy separation.

We are perfect for each other.

Right? I mean, I had seen it in my dream. I had had *the knowing*. She appeared within five minutes of my arrival.

Surely it is meant to be. Surely it was written.

We hang out for three hours, exploring, leaning into the truth of each other. Leaning in, closing and intensifying the pull of the magnet. It is glorious. Then I ask her a question that reveals a portal of her life that she isn't eager to share. She has been enjoying the dance, the whirling, the ecstasy of connection. And now, with my question, the answer spinning on the surface of her lips, the music screeches to a halt. The dance was over.

She is married.

The spell is broken.

I am broken.

We continued to hang out for the rest of the weekend. I sober up, no longer floating in the deep intoxication of possibility. Now I am like a younger brother—someone to love, but not to be in love with. The Friend Zone of pain and longing and suffering. Too close to look away. Too far to hold.

The plane ride home is full of introspection and poetry. The sunset is sympathetic, glowing and changing colors in full glory, trying to cheer me up.

I wonder how I could have been so stupid. What did I miss? I was trying to listen! "Gaaaaaaaahhhhhhh!"

I do not have rage for the Universe.

I have longing.

I have tapped into something so deep, so pure. So close, but not quite. I sense that it is all *right there*, if I can just decode the mystery. If I can listen.

I am close.

I feel the pull of the other half of the magnet.

A FEW months later I'm at a wine tasting party on a Friday night, hosted by two of my friends.

One of the hosts is named Bill. Most of us in our friend group are from somewhere else, not from Dallas. Bill is a local from Fort Worth. He is smart as hell and works at one of the tech companies in town. Where Bill is from, Bill is a two-syllable word.

Bee-yull.

His father was a cowboy. On the weekends Bill wears a western shirt with pressed jeans, a big belt buckle, and boots. And a serious cowboy hat. He has a ready, warm smile and a friendly drawl. He talks and dresses one hundred percent cowboy.

Bill's "momma" was from China. Bill looks one hundred percent Asian. Listening to Bill talk makes my head hurt. My brain can't compute his face and his voice together. It feels like I am watching one of those old Kung Fu movies that has been dubbed into English, but in this case his words match his lips perfectly.

We have a lot of laughs. Bill is a good dude. And he has brought a lot of friends from his company. I have rushed from work. I haven't even been thinking much about women. Yet.

Devin, the other host, knows that twenty-three-year-olds don't know much about wine. He is going to help with our education. We have all brought bottles of ten-dollar wine. Devin hides the labels, numbers them, and pours out little shots of each into tiny plastic cups. Communion for sinners. We each have a scorecard to rate our samples. At the end we'll see if we have learned anything about wine, if we had a favorite varietal, or if we cared.

I get up to grab the next round of samples. I ask a couple of young ladies near me if they want one. They shake their heads and go back to their conversation. Not interested. From behind them I hear, "I'll have one." A petite young woman with medium-length black hair looks up.

"Okay, got it."

I return with our wine samples.

"I think this is number six. Can you tell the difference?" I smile. I can't.

Her eyes sparkle in a way that makes me glow. We talk for the rest of the party. She says her name is Aparna. I have to say it a couple of times to get it right. She is beautiful. I can't place her ethnicity. Native American? Persian? Ecuadorian? No. Not quite.

She is from India. Moved to the U.S. when she was nine.

I like her. She is calm, in a deep way. My nervous system relaxes when I stand near her. Her eyes convey an intelligence, a wisdom, a knowing that is missing from most twenty-somethings. She is a software engineer. She has tried skydiving. She likes to travel. She likes adventure. She has a hunger for life. She has a sparkle in her eyes.

I play it cool. I don't ask for her number. I know I can get it from Bill if it is going to work out.

When the wine is done, I leave with my friends to go to the clubs and dance. I am lighter, cracking jokes in the car, shouting randomly. Happy. I tell my friends I have met someone.

On Monday I get her number from Bill. On Tuesday I call her and offer to make her dinner at my apartment. Apparently, she's hungry and doesn't want to cook, so she says yes.

She watches while I make dinner. Pasta primavera. We are easy together. I can feel the walls coming down. My insides start to settle. I can be myself. When I share some of my beliefs that had been so foreign in my hometown, she just nods. They are familiar to her. I play my guitar and sing her a song that I wrote about a whirling dervish. She smiles.

She sparkles.

On Thursday we have another date. We go to the movies, hunkered down in our seats, leaning in. I have no idea what the movie is. It could be a dog food commercial and it would still be perfection. It feels like we have known each other for a lifetime. For many lifetimes.

On Friday morning I tell my friends I'm going to marry her. They laugh so hard.

Eight weeks later I buy the ring. They laugh again, but in a different way this time. They can't believe it. They think I've lost my mind.

A few weeks after that we are engaged.

A few months later we are married.

When you know, you know.

I had The Full Body Yes. There was no doubt. Oh, sure, sometimes the mind would take over, would ask all the right logical questions. "Are you sure? It's only been a few weeks! You haven't even spent all of the seasons together. What if you don't like her in winter?"

I saw the signs. I listened very carefully. And then there was the difference between wanting and knowing. The difference between longing for the answer and knowing the answer. I was learning to listen to that voice and determine the difference. To feel it in my bones.

This time I knew. I had listened.

I had heard.

The isolation. The longing. The deep loneliness of feeling different and disconnected. Unseen. Separated.

These all disappeared when I was with Aparna.

This time I was home.

## Sit Quietly and Do Something: Listen

That inner voice makes itself known in a few different ways. Sometimes it smacks us in the head with its truth, like a parent who has asked their video-gamed zombie son to take out the trash for the eighth time in twenty minutes.

Usually it's subtle.

Also, it works for those who believe that it works. And for those who don't believe it works, it works that way as well.

It can come in a dream.

It can come in a waking dream. Bits of overheard conversation. Billboards. License plates. Fortune cookies. Signals in plain sight. They light up briefly with a golden-tongued wisdom. They appear if we are open.

Or, we get the knowing—The Full Body Yes. We just know.

When these messages come, we learn to distinguish them from the mind. This takes practice. The mind believes what it wants to believe. To be in tune with The Voice means to be in tune with that deeper part of ourselves. To be in tune with something beyond our own known borders.

To be in tune, to be able to sing along, we've got to listen.

## Without the Mastery of Me, We Have Stagnation

When we let go of our victimhood and take responsibility for our life, we put our feet squarely on the path toward freedom. Freedom is an inside job. It is not dependent on our external circumstances. We're not waiting for someone else to bring us the key. We make our own escape.

If we move our perspective from "life happens *to* us" to "life happens *for* us," then every experience is a chance to grow, to build capability. A chance to learn how to love more. A chance to "win."

It's a whole new game.

## PART IV

# Compassion in Action

The finest souls are those
who gulped pain and avoided making
others taste its bitterness.

**NIZAR QABBANI**

# 14

# AWARENESS OF OTHERS

"YOU'RE GONNA NEED to make that right."

My cousin and my two brothers are with my dad in the car. They have been to town running errands. My cousin from Omaha has been staying with us for the summer after he graduated from high school. He is nearly the same age as my brothers. For a kid from the city, farm life offers a form of adventure. Dirt bikes. Hunting. The responsibility and danger of working. The wide-open spaces.

Freedom.

"Aww, sweet!" My cousin is looking through his small bag of purchases from the general store.

"What?" says my brother.

"I just made ten bucks!" He is grinning like Mr. Moneybags from Monopoly.

"What? How's that?"

"My stuff was $6.50. I gave the guy ten bucks. He gave me $13.50 in change." He looked pleased, beaming at his good fortune, imagining the bounty.

"Ah, he thought you gave him a twenty."

The car starts to slow. My dad looks at my cousin in the rearview mirror. There is a pause.

"You're gonna need to make that right." He locks eyes with my cousin, makes sure he is being heard. An uncomfortable wave of tension washes through the car.

That's it. There will be no further lecture, no follow-up at the dinner table a week later. My dad will not drive my cousin back to the store. My dad will not remind him the next time they are in town together. It is up to my cousin to make it right.

My father has provided the tension between what is right and what is easy.

My dad goes by Ed. His full name is George Edward, but I never heard anyone call him George. He was named after his grandfather, George Emerson Shute. George Emerson had come to homestead the land in the 1880s. Back then there was nothing permanent but a sea of prairie grass and the wind. No trees, no buildings, no roads.

Each homestead was 160 acres. A quarter of a square mile. Over time, there was a family on each quarter. You knew your neighbors. The men helped each other with the farming. They'd build houses and buildings together. They'd harvest the wheat together. They'd borrow equipment. They'd lean on each other when times were hard. Times were hard a lot.

In the summer the women would can the vegetables together. They'd harvest the apricots, the chokecherries, and the mulberries together and make jam. They'd dress chickens. In the winter they'd get together to make quilts. They watched each other's children. They'd take turns housing the teacher of the single-room schoolhouse. They were connected.

This thread of connection runs deep in my father's veins. He has known the man at the hardware store for forty years. Even if he doesn't *know* him, he knows him. He knows how hard it is to scratch out a living in this place. He knows that what goes around comes around.

He knows who the ten dollars belongs to.

The tension my father provides stays with my cousin. It guides him in decision after decision as he grows into a man. It guides him when he teaches his own children. From that small seed it grows like a giant cottonwood tree inside of him, stretching his character. Straightening and strengthening his back. He becomes solid and tall. Rooted in something deeper.

Forty years later, at my father's funeral, my cousin tells this story, with the reverence of someone describing the creation of fire.

The memory, the tension my father provided, has shaped his life. Has guided him to create his own connections to those around him. He knows who the ten dollars belongs to.

It is just far too late to give it back.

## The Good Samaritan

Would you stop for a person in need?

That's the question that John Darley and Daniel Batson, professors of psychology and theology from Princeton, asked in a study called "From Jerusalem to Jericho" in 1973.[9] They centered their study on the parable Jesus tells of the Good Samaritan.

The story goes something like this.

A man, a Jew, a Levite, is traveling from Jerusalem to Jericho. On his journey, he falls in with robbers. They beat him badly, strip him of his clothes, take everything he has, and leave him half dead along the side of the road. Another man comes along, a fellow Levite. This merchant sees the beaten man on the side of the road. He looks pretty rough. The Levite is meeting another merchant in the next town. He needs to keep moving to make it on time and make his sale. He continues on his journey.

A priest passes through. He also sees the beaten traveler along the side of the road. He's nervous. He wonders if whoever has done this to the man is still around. He knows it is a busy road. Surely someone more capable will come along and help. Finally, a Samaritan, a man from a different tribe, comes along. In that day, Samaritans and Levites didn't care much for each other. He sees the beaten man at the side of the road. He sees the need. He is moved with compassion. He treats the man's wounds. He gathers him up on his own animal and brings him to the next town. He takes care of the Levite at an inn for the night. The next day the Samaritan gives the innkeeper some money to care for the man until he is back on his feet and can travel again. He tells the innkeeper to spend whatever is necessary to take care of the man. The Samaritan will pay him back when he passes back through town.

This is a classic story about compassion. It's a story every seminary student knows well. It's a story that every kid going to Sunday school and synagogue knows by the time they're six.

Darley and Batson were curious men. They wanted to know if the lessons these young seminary students were being taught were sinking in. Were the teachings really transforming these young men? Or was there something more to the story?

They had a plan.

They ran an experiment. They split a group of forty volunteers into two halves. The first half would record a short talk on the story of the Good Samaritan. The second group would record a short talk on the subject of job opportunities. The young men would prepare their talks in one building and then walk down a series of hallways and alleyways to another building, where they would perform their talk. Then the group was divided again. For part of the group, they gave "low hurry" instructions. Something like, "Okay, Jim, you can make your way over to the other room. If you leave now, you'll be a bit early. You can take your time." Another part of the group was given time pressure. Something like, "Oh, wow, I lost track of time. Jim, you're already late. They'll be waiting for you. You'd better get over there now." Each was given a sketch showing how to reach the other office: out the front door, turn right, go into the alley at the right, then first left.

As the young students each made their way to the other building, turning right, right again... they found a young man lying in a doorway in the alley.

The researchers had staged a scene with their own "victim," an actor portraying a man who was in distress. He was coughing and moaning and looked like he was in pain.

He needed help.

To reach their destination the students had to walk right past this man in need. In some cases, to get by, they would need to step over the victim, the actor. These students were all pious young men. Earnest. On the brink of fulfilling their mission. They were all in search of their deeper truth. Every one of them had been called to a life of service, a life of inquiry about their own true nature, the nature of love. Nearly every Sunday for the rest of their lives they would be talking about compassion. Surely each one of them in their training had pleaded with the Universe to provide them with opportunities to serve. They had imagined people in need. They had imagined their hearts being open and their gifts on full display as they helped those poor people.

Surely each one of them would stop and help the man in distress in the courtyard.

Look in your own heart, to your own experience, and you already know the answer.

It made almost no difference which talk the men were preparing to give. The men who were given time pressure were *six times less likely* to stop and help. Their good intentions had been hijacked by their amygdala. The lizard brain had taken over.

They needed to be in the other building on time. They were focused on me, me, me.

In some cases, they were headed to tell their story about the Good Samaritan, highlighting the virtues of helping a man in need. On the way to give that talk they literally stepped over a man in need, lying in a doorway in the alley.

Each of them were good people. In their quiet moments each of them visualized being selfless. Each of them had good intentions.

Time.

Time is a pressure that pulls the blinders down on our awareness.

Time is a pressure that our good intention yields to.

## The Elders

When I was a kid I would tag along with my mom as she ran errands in town. In addition to the groceries and the general store, one of the regular stops was to visit the "old people," as I called them. For years, my mother kept this practice, regular as the moon. First, there was dad's Aunt Grace in the nursing home, then later my Grandma Alice. These weren't even her own blood relatives, but my mom was there every few days to check in on them and make conversation when they were able to. Or even if they weren't. She'd talk to them through their fog, sharing news of the farm, news of the neighborhood. She would bring them pie and cookies and other goodness from her kitchen. For years and years, she visited them. It was one of those largely invisible, quiet, selfless acts that define her life. She is a saint.

I hated this part. I hated the smell of the nursing home. I hated the frozen pace of life. I hated the fading energy of the place. I did not want to be there. I just wanted to be outside and free. As an eight-year-old I'm sure I didn't make it any easier on my mom.

One of the stops on our journey was to visit my Great-Grandpa AJ. He lived to be one hundred. Lived by himself in a tiny little house. Got his driver's license renewed when he was ninety-six. It seemed to me like he had been ancient forever. He was born in the 1800s. He had a colorful history, piecing together a living with a hundred different jobs, including, most interestingly, running a mortuary. He led a brass band in the early 1900s, during the time of John Philip Sousa, whose band came to town one summer. He played trombone. Our family traces our musical ability back through my mom, through my Grandma Allene, who was a church pianist for over eighty years, to my Grandpa AJ. He had life in his veins. He had a sparkle in his eyes. Of all the elders, he was my favorite. He was everyone's favorite.

When my mom would reach into a bag and retrieve a piece of her famous cherry pie, his face would glow as if he'd been handed a bar of solid gold. My siblings and I would beg him to tell stories of the supernatural things he had seen during his time as a mortician. Stories for which there were no earthly explanations. Sometimes he would reach back into his memory banks and share his wonder. Mostly, he made it about us. He'd ask questions about my life. About how I was doing, what I was interested in. He looked deeply into my eyes. He listened to what I was saying. He was present. He made me feel special. He saw me.

I never complained when we visited Grandpa AJ. He was less interested in reliving his past. He was more interested in living in the present through us.

## Ronan

"We need to work on your executive presence."

It's annual review time. Performance reviews. I'm not looking forward to this one. Ronan has been leading the team in Dublin for a couple of years. He is popular with his team. He is gregarious. He has their backs. He is young and talented and ambitious. He can also be loud and abrasive. He has been getting mixed reviews from the regional managing director and the leadership team in Europe. He is polarizing. Some see him only as a customer support manager, not as a leader or a peer. Some see his great potential and have patience with his rawness.

I have been managing him from five thousand miles and eight time zones away. My interactions have largely been limited to video calls. Our relationship is tough over video. The boisterousness he shows with others turns serious and firm with me. He often scowls at me through the monitor.

I try not to take it personally. Try to assume that he is just more guarded with me because of my position, not because of me as a person. But still, the scowling doesn't help. I have all kinds of stories in my mind of what the scowling is about.

Going over his annual review, I share all of the positives. Review his successes. Compliment his strengths. The list is long. Then we get to the "could be improved" section. This is complicated. The feedback from the senior leaders in the office is vague. Something is missing. He isn't quite there yet, but they can't tell me what it is. If he is going to be promoted to director, I need these leaders to be on board. They need to be fans of Ronan.

I need them to be fans of me as well. They are my peers. They are very influential. How they feel about Ronan is a proxy for how they feel about me.

Ronan desperately wants the promotion. He feels strongly that he deserves it. He has expected it this round. When I share a copy of his review with him and the promotion is not part of it, his scowl increases in intensity. He is heated. *Why?* he wants to know.

I can feel the blood rising in my face. Conflict is not my strength. Some people enjoy it. They thrive on it. My life strategy is likeability. My strength is in alignment. I can do conflict, but it takes a lot out of me. It's not natural for me. I don't like it.

"We need to work on your executive presence."

Ronan tilts his head, takes it in. He knows where this feedback is coming from. The more senior members in the office haven't all warmed up to him. He has been trying to win them over but keeps running into roadblocks. He is irritated that his career is being held up by others.

"And what does that mean, exactly?" His eyes, even through the video call, are piercing.

I start talking, but the words are empty. I don't have much to say. He doesn't push further.

My mind churns on our conversation for days. Ronan is at a critical junction in his career. The stakes are high.

I have failed him.

I am disgusted with myself. His career is being held up and I can't give him a direct reason why. In my own busyness, and focusing on my own story, I have not done the very hard work of digging in. Digging deeper with the other leaders. Digging deeper with my own opinions and perceptions. The other leaders are very likely in the same boat. Each of them is incredibly busy. Each of them is trying to get along, to be cordial. It's so much easier and less confrontational to have a vague judgment versus a deeply thought-out, structured opinion. I have no actionable feedback, other than "You're not quite ready" and "We need to work on your executive presence."

I remember, nearly twenty years earlier, the performance conversation that Adam once had with me.

*I need more from you.*

*What does that mean?*

*I don't know . . . I just need more from you.*

I remember the frustration and anger and sense of impotence that left me with. Now it has come full circle. I am sitting on the other side of the table, doing the exact same thing.

I imagine it from Ronan's perspective. I imagine him going back to his desk, staring at his email. Wondering what to do next. I can feel his frustration.

I vow to do better. I push through my discomfort.

After my meeting with Ronan I dive deeper into the conversations with the senior leaders in Dublin and London. I get uncomfortable. I push through. I challenge them. When their comments are vague, I challenge them. My back stiffens. I challenge them to mentor him, to invest in him. I challenge them to give specific, actionable feedback. Otherwise, I say, I have to ignore it.

I ask them this question: "What would need to be true for Ronan to have your support for a promotion?"

They consider. They also commit to the hard work of tough conversations.

I apologize to Ronan. I let him know that I have his back. I let him know that I am going to do a better job of providing more real-time and actionable feedback. I will push the leadership team in Dublin to be better mentors as well. In turn, if he can rise to the occasion, if he can listen to our feedback with humility and respond well, he will be successful.

My own insecurities have gotten in the way of being a good leader. I have been focused on building a relationship with the other senior leaders—I haven't wanted to rock the boat. I have been too focused on trying to build a relationship with Ronan.

I haven't wanted to have hard conversations with him. I have been playing to my strengths, focusing on collaboration and connection, only to expose a gaping weakness.

So I get out of my own way, get more comfortable being uncomfortable. I become a better leader.

Ronan receives great, actionable feedback from the leadership team on the ground, and better feedback from me. By engaging him in real conversation they get to know him in a different way, see him in a different light. They become fans. I dig in and come up with a real definition for executive presence, one that I am able to use more broadly in the organization.

Compassion is not weak. To be able to be aware of another and to take action on their behalf can take enormous strength. Sometimes it requires a difficult conversation. Sometimes we have to get out of our own way. We might have to get uncomfortable. Sometimes it requires us to learn a new set of tools.

Nine months later Ronan is promoted to director. Dropping the posturing, becoming more vulnerable, and digging into these hard conversations does not damage our relationship—it makes it stronger. We learn how to best work with each other. Ronan becomes one of my highest-performing, most-trusted lieutenants. Over time we become friends.

And Ronan's scowl of disgust with me over video?

Turns out Ronan needs glasses. He has been squinting because he can't see me otherwise.

## Just Listen

Compassion doesn't have to be complicated. As humans, one of our deepest held needs is the need to be seen. To be heard. To be acknowledged. To be gotten. Sometimes the most powerful thing we can do is to just listen. To see the other person.

To hold space for them as they express themselves, as they take steps on their own journey to their True Self.

## The Phone Call

"Kumiko is going to take me to the doctor."

My wife is on the phone. I'm sitting at my desk at work. We've been living in Tokyo for six months as part of a two-year work assignment. It's been a challenge for Aparna. She's temporarily given up her career so that we can keep our growing family intact. She doesn't speak much Japanese. Our son, Kameron, is two years old. It's not easy to get around. Everything is different.

"Are you okay?" I ask.

"I think so. I went to the bathroom and I was bleeding." She says this matter-of-factly. I'm trying to read her tone.

"I think I might have lost the baby." There is a catch in her voice.

I am numb. Frozen. I don't know what to say or do. She is ten weeks pregnant. It is still early. I am still adjusting to the thought of having a second child. I have barely been keeping up with the pace of our current life.

"I'm sorry." I pause, for a long time. It's quiet. I have no words. "Is there anything I can do?"

"Kumiko is going to take me to the doctor. I'll call you after that." I can hear her go into action mode. She's a planner. She gets stuff done. She would be getting Kameron ready, packing up what she needed. Being efficient.

"Okay, I'm sorry." Long pause. "I'll talk to you later."

I stare out the office window from the eighteenth floor. On a clear day I can see Mt. Fuji's snowy peak. I am leading a customer operations function for an American company. We are trying to build our presence in Asia. I am thirty-one. All of the managers on my team, mostly Japanese, are older than me. I have been sent to build a team in Tokyo, and in Shanghai. This job, this experience, is a dream come true. I had once been an exchange student in Japan and have been looking for a way to return. The company is paying a fortune for us to live in a three-bedroom apartment in central Tokyo. To live like westerners. Most of my team live a ninety-minute train ride away in tiny one-bedroom apartments. I feel guilty about it. I am determined to be worth it.

In Japan it is customary to work long hours, often until 8 or 9 p.m., sometimes followed by business meetings that extend until the trains stopped running at midnight. In this society, in this work environment, there is extraordinary pressure to conform. They value the group. The needs of the individual are secondary.

"The nail that sticks out will get hammered back in."

I feel the weight of it.

I have already been stressing the system. I had been used to working in Silicon Valley. Flex time. Focus on the individual. Work-life balance. In Tokyo, I am the first one to arrive unseen in the office in the morning. I have early meetings with my manager and peers in California. I try to leave the office each day by six. Try to keep some focus on the family I have led across the Pacific. I decline as many drinking evenings as I can. Every time I leave the office, I can feel eyes watching me. Judging me.

I am meant to be here for two years. They all know it. I am trying to get a lot done. Make a lot of changes. Changes that had been designed in California, but have to be implemented here in Tokyo, where continuity and history have a more treasured place than change. Some welcome the change. Some just stall, waiting out the two years until I leave.

I am caught in the middle. I am at the center of the tear in the fabric.

Aparna is strong. She's capable. Any task that comes up, she jumps into action. She handles things. She is a doer. She has taken care of everything at home so I can do what I need to at work. She's given up her own career, her own ambitions, so I can live mine. I've taken that for granted. She's so capable and I have so many other challenges that I am often blind to her needs.

That evening there's a special dinner event that I'm supposed to lead. My team has arranged for me to meet with the senior leadership team from a key partner, our distributor. They are important players in the changes I'm trying to implement. It has taken us a long time to find dates that work. We need them more than they need us. These men are thirty years my senior. We will lose face if I don't go.

I will lose face if I don't go.

I'm at the restaurant, in a private room with their leadership team. Everyone is just arriving. We're sitting on a tatami mat while beers and appetizers are making their way to the table. My phone rings. It's Aparna.

Eyebrows raise as I excuse myself.

"Hi hon. You okay?"

"I'm *okay*. I'm fine." There's a long pause. I can tell she's not quite fine.

"I lost the baby." More long pause.

"Oh no. I'm so sorry." I'm frozen. I don't know what to say. Waitresses are passing me in the hallway. There's noise from other parties getting started.

More silence.

"Is there anything I can do?" It's quiet and awkward, while the noise and buzz of the restaurant surrounds me.

"I'm just . . . here." More quiet. More awkward. I have a thousand thoughts at once and none of them seem to be useful.

"I'll be home as soon as I can." A wave of deep sadness and helplessness washes my energy away. I'm numb.

More silence.

"Okay then."

I awkwardly end the call. I take a deep breath and head back into the meeting. I try to focus. It feels like I've been punched in the stomach. Tears are close by. I try to smile and say the right things. I try to speak in Japanese as much I can, careful not to mix up my words. Nothing happens quickly. We don't start talking about business until two hours later. Even then, it's more exploratory. We don't actually get anything done or decided. This is how it goes here. Relationships first, business second. Trust has to be earned. They're testing me. I'm trying to find a good time to bow out.

There isn't one.

I shouldn't be here.

The meeting takes too long. I ride the train home late, exhausted.

Twenty years later, it's so easy to see. I should have come home as soon as Aparna called the first time. I should have asked my team to reschedule the meeting. I should have heard the fear in my wife's voice. Put myself in her shoes. Realized how terrifying it would be to go to a Japanese hospital and get examined by a male doctor who speaks no English. Understood the isolation that she would feel, so far from home, so far from friends, so far from anything that might comfort her. Realized the sadness she would feel at the loss of the life growing inside of her.

I should have seen that, yet instead of being there to comfort her, I was part of the situation that was causing her pain.

I had abandoned her.

If those things had been clearer. If I had recognized all of that, the decision would have been easier. If somehow life had held up a sign and said, "Look, stop what you're doing. This is one of the most important moments of your whole life. You need to be there. Right now!" Then yes, of course, I'd snap to life. I'd come to my senses and rush to her side.

In fact, life *was* trying to tell me. The signs were there, but I had kept a lead foot through all the red lights.

*I had not been aware of Aparna's needs because I am stuck in my own story.*

In my story I am torn at work. I have no time. I feel like I'm always behind, like I'm already not doing enough. I am already stretched thin being a father, being a leader, being a husband. I have commitments. Plans that need to work out. Expectations that need to be exceeded, not just met. In a game of musical chairs, I have been trying to please far more people than I have chairs for. And something deeper, hidden, shameful. I'm not sure if I am ready for another child. I am afraid.

I am deep in my own pressures. My own story. My own struggle. My own fear.

Me. Me. Me.

This obsession with my own story means that I have been deaf to Aparna's story. To her pain. I can't see it.

I have failed.

I have failed to listen. Failed to be aware.

I have failed in a way that caused my partner pain. Pain that runs deep and has never quite healed.

Trust has to be earned.

Each of us faces choices between our commitments every day. Some days it's easy to choose. Some days it seems impossible. It's a running game of compromise. Sometimes it's appropriate to choose work. Sometimes we need to prioritize family. It starts with being aware. Getting out of our own story. Putting ourselves in the other person's shoes.

Sometimes the learning comes easy. Sometimes wisdom is learned through suffering and failure.

With the benefit of time and experience, I understand that I was making a lot of assumptions about what my Japanese colleagues and business partners would think. I could have simply and confidently explained that there was a family emergency and asked to reschedule. I'm sure they would have understood. Like many problems, the drama was largely in my mind.

This lesson is one I'm still learning. It's been a long and painful lesson, one that I seem to come back to time and time again. There is clearly something in my history, my makeup, that is deeply rooted. Patterns that are resistant to change. Life systems that are designed to meet certain goals. Goals that I'm questioning more and more. Here's what I'm still learning.

I'm learning that, fifteen years from now, the jobs we're completely consumed by in this moment will likely be reduced to three bullets on a resume. Our relationships, the connections with our family, our colleagues, our neighbors—those will be with us forever.

Our achievements at work may be the way that society, the way *others*, define us.

Those connections, those achievements of the heart, will be the way we define our own success in the end.

Part of me has been keeping score wrong this whole time.

## How Compassion Starts

Are there areas in your life where you'd like to demonstrate more compassion?

Compassion starts with being aware of others. We're usually so caught up in our own lives that we become blind to the needs of those around us.

How are they feeling? What's most important for them?

Our own problems, our own internal struggles, are a constant hum of distraction. This distraction keeps us from noticing what's going on with others.

Once we get ourselves out of the way, how do we build that awareness?

We start by being present. We get curious.

We listen.

A truce to your volumes,

your studies, give o'er:

For books cannot teach you

love's marvelous lore.

**HAFIZ**

# 15

# COMPASSION
# FOR OTHERS

IT'S AUGUST. HOT. Saturday afternoon. I'm mowing the lawn. My mind is busy. It's busy with the work piling up for the following week. It's busy with the argument I had with a family member. It's busy with the lack of sleep from the night before. I'm tired and restless and just plain over it.

I go back and forth on my tiny lawn, strips of darker and lighter green appearing. I'm irritated, tossing the mower around on the turns, huffing. I don't want to be here, mowing the lawn. I also don't want to be here, in my head, with this frustration.

Malcontent.

To add to my frustration, I have self-judgment. Why am I so angry? Why can't I just snap out of it? Why? It seems like it should be easier than this. I know better. But still, here I am, pushing the mower like it bit me and I'm getting my revenge. In my haste I get a little too close to the flower bed and take out a happy little section of marigolds. There's a ragged tear where I've been. Now their little choir is missing the tenor section.

I remember something my teacher once said. People come to him; they write letters asking for advice. Their problems seem insurmountable. They're stuck. They always want to know: "What do I do?"

He said he used to write them back and lay out the whole story, show them how they got into the mess in the first place, then give them some steps to make things better. But most aren't ready for that kind of truth, he found. They're not ready to see themselves that clearly.

Instead, now he writes back with only one piece of advice.

*When you're stuck, do one thing each day out of pure love, pure service, with no expectation of reward.*

This is on my mind as I push the mower around. I need a release. I am willing to try it.

I notice the lawn across the street. It belongs to Robert. I remember that Robert has been having a hard time. His mother passed away. He's had a knee replaced. He hasn't been feeling well. His lawn is becoming overgrown.

"Okay," I think. "No big deal. I'll mow Robert's lawn when I'm done."

It's simple. When I finish my lawn, I just cross the street and start mowing. It's been awhile. The grass is tall. The mower complains, so I raise the deck.

As I mow, I think more about Robert. We've never really hit it off. He keeps to himself. He's kind of gruff. He doesn't appreciate my kids making noise in the street. Doesn't like it when a stray ball travels into his yard. Mostly, we avoid each other.

I wonder how he's doing. If he has had any visitors. If he misses his mother. I wonder if he has any siblings to talk to. I hope he is feeling better, that he is healing nicely.

I am starting to feel better. I am starting to heal nicely.

I didn't expect him to thank me. I didn't expect that he'd come out with a plate of cookies and lemonade, though the thought makes me chuckle. It isn't that big of a deal. Takes me five minutes.

I am feeling better. Lighter.

Something about the act of giving has released the tension of my own troubles.

A miracle cure.

Life seems backward sometimes. I was miserable. Then I did something that I don't like to do for someone I don't really care for.

And *that* has made me happy.

## The Elephant

A group of blind men were sitting in the sun one day when they heard a ruckus. There was activity in the courtyard. They could feel the place stirring. Murmurs among strangers. Shouts among friends. The air was electric with possibility. They could smell the dust in the air as children ran past them.

"What's happening?" one of them said to a passerby who could see.

"There's an elephant in the courtyard," the man replied and continued on his way.

The men caucused among themselves.

"An elephant? What's an elephant?" None of them knew. They had never heard of such a beast. They had been largely content sitting as they had done day after day, chatting about nothing and everything. But now there was a buzz. A delicious purr of possibility. They needed to know.

They decided to venture to the courtyard to experience the elephant. They hoped they'd be able to touch it, perhaps to hear it, to see it with all of their senses without sight.

They wove their way through the crowds. They followed their ears to the source. They heard the animal's heavy footsteps, grunting breaths, and occasional trumpet. The crowd pressed in around them. They became separated. Now each man was on a sacred, independent journey for the truth.

Each of them eventually made it to the animal. Their hands explored the elephant with the care of a jeweler, the soft touch of a lover. They absorbed knowledge through their fingers. Wonder filled their hearts.

After a bit the elephant's handler grew impatient. It was time to move on. The entourage migrated away from the men. They could hear the procession move beyond their touch.

Satisfied, they smiled.

They made their way back to their little padded corner of the courtyard, excited to share their experience, giddy with sensation.

"What a wonder!"

"So exciting."

"Amazing."

"Fantastic."

"I didn't anticipate that. So different than I imagined."

"Indeed."

"I didn't realize that an elephant would be so hard and pointy. Like a spear."

"Wait, what? No, no. The elephant was thin and wide, flexible like a fan!"

"I don't know what you two are talking about. The elephant was strong and tall and flat, like the side of a building. Like a wall." The conversation was starting to get heated.

"Fools! It was soft and curvy like a giant serpent."

"I don't know where you were. You're confused. The elephant was like the trunk of a tree."

Shouting erupted between the men. They were incredulous. Each was indignant, knowing full well that they alone were in fact correct. It would only be a matter of time before the others' ignorance was unveiled.

They argued deep into the night.

Distrust started to creep into their thoughts. Why would the others lie about such things? How can they be so incredibly dense? They questioned the very foundations of their friendships. Walls of mistrust began to form. The men became withdrawn.

Their hearts closed to each other.

Their relationships were never the same.


## Three Steps

My friend David once shared with me his three-step process of how to change other people. This is incredibly useful, because there seem to be *a lot* of people in the world that I'd like to change. They can be irritating. Annoying. Frustrating. You know exactly what I mean. You have them in your life as well.

So... here you go. Write this one down and keep it in your pocket. Here are three steps that will change your life.

First, imagine this person that annoys you so much. Think about the behavior that is irritating, that thing they're doing that you so dislike.

Name it. Really get a sense of how it makes you feel.

(Pause here and actually think about it. Feel it.)

Next, think about all the times in your life that you've done something similar. Try to recall as many of these as you can.

Some of your behaviors will be exactly the same as the person you're struggling with. Some will be slightly different. If you look carefully, there will be many. Think about how others around you have felt when you have acted that way.

(Pause here to think about the impact you've had on others.)

Third...

There is no third step!

We're programmed to
only feel compassion for
those who are like us.
The good news is that
it's not hard-wired.
We can change.

## Hands

David Eagleman is a neuroscientist from Stanford. He and his team did some fascinating research that was shared on his show, *The Brain with David Eagleman*.[10] They put people in an MRI machine and studied their brains while the participants were watching a video. The video was of a human hand. From the corner of the screen you see a giant syringe. It comes closer to the hand until it finally pierces the skin in that meaty place between the thumb and index finger.

You might guess the response. As participants, we might wince. We might exclaim something out loud, like, "Ewww, ouch!" It's kind of like when we watch a scary movie. The lead character, a young woman, is in a dark house. For apparently no reason at all, she's about to open the door of an old, rickety closet. We're pretty sure the creepy clown is hiding in there. As we watch, our bodies and our brains react, almost as if we're standing right there with her.

With the needle video, this is what the researchers found. When the participants watched the hand being stabbed with the syringe, the pain matrix in their brains lit up. They reacted. They felt something. They felt something for the other person, as if it were happening to them.

That was the control group.

In the next set of experiments, Eagleman and his team used six different hands. The hands were a selection of different skin tones. Each one had a label next to it. Hindu. Muslim. Christian. Scientologist. Atheist. Jew. At random, the participant was shown a video of a hand with a label getting stabbed. If the label of the hand was from the participant's "in group," their brain's pain matrix lit up. If the label was from the person's "out group," there was essentially no response.

A flat line.

In other words, we're programmed to feel for others from our "in group." We're programmed to not feel for people from our "out group." This feeling, seeing others as similar to us, plays a huge role in our ability to have compassion for others.

This is not about religion. It's about who we identify with. Whose team we're on.

Who we view as similar.

Over millions of years our species has evolved this way. In a resource-scarce environment, this is how we stayed alive. If we lived in a small valley with our tribe, it makes sense that we would protect our fellow tribe members. If a member of another tribe came to hunt on our territory or steal our tools or animals, we'd protect ourselves. We might resort to violence to stay alive.

That strategy may have worked well in that isolated, resource-scarce environment.

It fails us when we live in a highly interconnected world of seven billion people.

It fails us when we try to work together as a team or an organization.

It fails us most of the time.

We see this play out on the evening news. We can see how divided the world is. Politics. Race. Ideology. With social media and specialized news outlets, our opinions are solidified. Our division is amplified. Our capacity for compassion is eroded.

That's the bad news. We're programmed to only feel compassion for those who are like us.

The good news is that it's not hard-wired. It's programmed. It's conditioning. It can be changed.

We can change.

## Wi-Fi of the Heart

It's week fourteen of the COVID-19 quarantine. We're shelter-
ing in place. Before this time, we've never used this phrase.
Now it's become the norm. I'm in about the 364th Zoom call
I've had over this time.

The world is breaking. First comes years of political divide,
now escalating during an election year. I read CNN and then
Fox News and wonder which of the two planets I live on. Then
the coronavirus ruins all of our plans and creates a new normal.
In this moment we have no idea what the future holds. When
we'll go back to work. When daycare will open. When we can
eat in a restaurant. When we can shake hands or hug. Then
Minneapolis and George Floyd hits the news, and the storm
of racial injustice and tension boils over and more change is
added to the change.

The world is breaking to form something new. Something
better.

We hope.

There are thirty-five of us on the Zoom call for a group meeting. We're having an open meeting to share our thoughts about
racial injustice. It's been a tense and exhausting week. Our
Black teammates have especially suffered greatly. Each of us
is experiencing something different, based on our own unique
cocktail of experiences. We are questioning our own beliefs.
Some of us feel guilt. Some of us are distracted and over-
whelmed with our own situations—trying to homeschool three
kids under ten years old while working full time. Some of us
wonder why it's taken so long for us to understand. To wake up.

On this call there is a great vulnerability displayed. A Black
colleague shares her story. She shares the day-to-day pain that
she endures. The microaggressions. How the neighbors ask
if she's the dog walker, even though she's lived with them in
the same apartment building for three years. How she gets

followed in a department store when she shops. How she comes to work rattled after Breonna Taylor is killed and is shocked and lost when realizing her white colleagues are not shocked or lost. Most are not even aware of the story. She wonders which of the two planets she lives on. She is nearly in tears. She speaks in a way that conveys the depths of her experience and emotion, while also giving the rest of us grace to live and value our own experiences.

We are all fully present. We are making eye contact. No one is reading their email. No one is texting under the table. No one is shopping on Amazon. No one is multitasking, half paying attention to the little squares of people on our monitors.

We're right there. We're present.

We're there with her as she walks her dog. We're there with her when she's shopping. We're crying with her at her desk. We're crying on this video call with her.

The meeting continues. Other people share their experiences. We're open. We're vulnerable. We're real.

The meeting is scheduled for forty-five minutes. We talk for two hours.

When it's over, people remark about how this has been the first time they felt that the technology didn't get in the way of the connection.

The connection!

People feel as if we'd never been more connected. As humans. The little boxes on the screen are equalizers. We're all at home in the mess of our lives. There are no private offices. There are no titles or levels or height differences. We're all equal-sized on the screen.

My friend calls this the Wi-Fi of the Heart. We don't need to be in the same space to feel connected to each other. We can tune in to each other.

The recipe is simple. It's not easy, but it's simple.

Be present. Listen. Be vulnerable. Assume good intentions. Lift each other up.

Simple.

Not easy.

## The Iceberg

Compassion at the deepest level requires us to truly wish the best for someone else.

To love them.

Unconditionally.

To comprehend love, I think of an iceberg. The tip of the iceberg, the part that sticks up out of the water—this is the part we allow other people to see. For some of us, or in some situations, that visible part is very small. We're closed off. When we share ourselves more, and when another person holds that space for us, it feels amazing. It feels so good that we want to share even more. We lower the waterline on our iceberg.

This is most obvious for me at parties. When I go to a party and don't know very many people, I often start off pretty guarded—just the tip of the iceberg showing.

I find myself standing by the food, maybe protecting the chips and dip.

The husband of one of my wife's friends is also there, grazing on the sliced bell peppers and hummus. We strike up a conversation. As we share our names and where we live, the waterline on our iceberg lowers a bit, we start to soften. If we keep the conversation at the surface level—kids, neighborhood news, weather—nothing much changes. This is a line that's well-worn on the iceberg. The sun nearly always shines here, and the exposed ice is weathered and hardened from experience. We have a nice conversation. It's fine. And... at the end of the evening I can barely remember the guy's name.

If we go a bit further and talk about something we're passionate about—our hobbies, say—the waterline drops a bit more. Maybe we bond over our love of the San Francisco Giants. We talk about spring training, and which of the new prospects will make it to the twenty-five-man big league roster by July. Maybe we share which mountain bike trails are best this time of year. I once spent an entire afternoon listening to a neighbor talk about the intricacies of beekeeping.

No one else at the party is interested. His wife occasionally drops by, then rolls her eyes and walks away when she hears how he is deep into his explanation of how the drone bees will all hover around the queen when it's cold, wings beating furiously just to keep her warm. His wife is in search of fresh material. I am enthralled. I ask more questions, show enthusiasm. I'm not faking it. I'm seriously interested, and the more questions I ask, the more excited he gets. He has gone deep into the world of bees. He loves it. He is lit up.

We talk bees for two hours. It doesn't take long for people around us to stare into their drinks, walk away to go reload, and not come back. It doesn't matter to us. We're content.

I guarantee you he went home that afternoon feeling lighter, happier. This love for bees was part of his creative expression, part of his identity. Most people don't care *that much* about bees. They might have a mild interest. They might like the honey. But they have no interest in talking about bees for two hours.

They might ask my friend about bees to start a conversation, having heard that he was a beekeeper. He might drop the waterline and start to share. But at some point, they're going to lose interest. They don't care to know more. If he misses the cues and continues on about his bees, at some point they'll just want him to stop talking. They'll shift the conversation. Or they'll lightly poke fun at him or his bees as a signal to move on. He's used to it. The waterline will go back up. The light will dim. He'll go get another drink. Start a conversation about the weather.

Often, the people in our lives that we're closest to are the ones where we've drawn the waterline the lowest. Maybe it's our high school or college friends—they've known us the longest. Because of our shared experiences, they've seen more of the iceberg below the surface. It could be friends that share one of our hobbies or passions. We've gone deep below the waterline together in certain areas: baseball, music, kids.

There's a special, deep bond with others with whom we've shared a difficult experience, or even a trauma. Maybe we both lost our fathers—and have a unique understanding of the grief, even though we weren't together at the time. Maybe we experienced abuse. Maybe we suffer because we have alcoholics in the family. Maybe we've experienced depression. Maybe we've gone through divorce. Maybe we've lost our jobs.

As we try to unpack these painful situations, searching for ways to heal ourselves, we are deeply appreciative of having these other people in our lives. We can share with them. We can unpack our burdens with them. They reflect our own experiences. They help us heal.

When we drop our waterline to expose the beginnings of the jagged, dark scar on our underbellies, they do not flinch. They understand. They get it. To prove their loyalty to our vulnerability, they share their own scar. We exhale, letting go of the tension of isolation. We're so relieved to finally find someone to tell our story to. We have needed to bring this scar into the light. They *get* us.

If we are so lucky as to find another person who we can share our *entire* iceberg with, someone we can bare our soul to, who will love us and appreciate us for all of our faults, as well as the entirety of our strengths, this is rare.

A treasure.

We typically don't even do this for ourselves. We have shame or disgust about the dark scars—the ugly parts of ourselves. It's hard enough to be honest and expose our full iceberg to our own light. To see it fully and to love it. To love ourselves.

Many of us only have this type of pure relationship with what we call the Divine. The Universe. The Whole. The One. God.

Whatever your name for it, or even if you believe in it, the feeling is the same. To have your entire being, rainbows and dark scars, fully exposed to the light. To be held with reverence. With understanding.

Unconditionally.

Poets search for words that might touch this feeling. Artists look for combinations of color that awaken and stir something deep within. Preachers and rabbis, imams and gurus—they're all searching for the words that might light this spark.

We can learn to give this to ourselves, unconditionally.

We can give it to each other, unconditionally.

We can begin to become aware that we are part of The Thing itself.

Here's how.

### Microcompassions

The opposite of microaggressions are microcompassions. These are actions we can take every day, every moment.

Microcompassions happen any time we're moving from *me* to *we*, any time we're lifting someone up, any time we're making connections. These are things we can do to consciously help someone else's light shine brighter.

### Smiling

It's not hard. When we're walking the dog. When we greet each other in a meeting. When we're in line at the grocery store. Just smile. Say hello.

## Compliments

This follows the smile. When we see someone, we can first smile at them. Then, we can notice something good about them. "Oh, I like your earrings." "Your shoes are cool." "I like what you said in the meeting last week." "I always appreciate seeing you."

## Inclusion

In a meeting we often hear only a few voices, while others remain quiet. We can bring the quiet ones into the fold. "Jane, I'd really like to hear what you have to say." Or if you're getting together with friends, is there someone who often doesn't get included who would like to be invited?

## Listening

Just listen, with the intention of deeply understanding the other person. Not thinking about your own story. Not waiting to interject. What are they trying to say, and why?

## Curiosity

What question can you ask that will light someone up? Get curious. Make it a point to remember. "Sanjay, how's that patio project coming?" "Lisa, what's your puppy up to this week?" "Colin, have you been surfing lately?" And my favorites: "What's most alive for you right now?" "What are you most grateful for today?"

COMPASSION DOESN'T have to be a big act. We can create a culture of compassion in our workplace, in our family, in our neighborhood, with simple gestures.

Here's a nice surprise: each of these, if we do them with an open heart, will make us feel better.

The best way to find yourself
is to lose yourself in the service of others.

**MAHATMA GANDHI**

# 16

# LIFE HAPPENS THROUGH US

I CAN'T REMEMBER!

I'm sitting in front of my desk, playing guitar. I have volunteered to play one of my original songs at a service on Sunday morning. It is Saturday night. This is the first time I have practiced since being asked to serve a few months ago.

I have all kinds of excuses. I've been busy. I've been distracted. I have a big job. I have family commitments.

And now, here I am, twelve hours before going onstage, and I can't remember how the song goes. This is a problem. I don't have a recording of it. I can't call a friend. I wrote it.

My inner talk track goes dark. And ugly.

First, there comes the critic.

"Oh, this is bad. What a failure! What are you thinking? Why are you just now starting to practice?"

Then comes the guilt.

"Ugh. There are people counting on you. This really sucks that you're going to let them down."

There is more: the ego jumps in, trying to protect itself.

"This is not my brand. What are people going to think of me?"

On and on. Spinning. The more I spin, the further away I get from remembering the song.

"Stop it!"

I nearly startle. The Voice is back, with a sharp command. It is so clear. I straighten my back. Put my guitar pick down on the desk in front of me. Take my hands off the guitar and hold them up in surrender. It has my attention.

I close my eyes.

Breathe.

Try to tune in to that higher part of me. The part that is infinite. The part that knows.

"We don't have time for your bullshit."

The Voice is very efficient. It speaks in a language that I understand. In an instant I get the whole lesson. If you're going to serve, serve. There's no room for the little self, the ego. There's no room for the ugly inner critic. Just serve. This is not about you.

Just.

Serve.

I take it in. As I breathe, I try to let go.

Yes, I am here to serve. I think, "Okay. Tomorrow morning I have five minutes onstage. Maybe it will evolve into a talk about procrastination. Maybe it will be funny in a way that is moving and memorable. Maybe it will collapse into a failure and become a lesson about humility. Whatever happens, I'm going there to serve."

I smile. I am ready for anything.

"*Okay*. Here we go."

After a few more deep breaths I start playing again. Bit by bit I remember the song. Bit by bit the words come back to me. It isn't polished, but it comes from a good place.

The next day I drive to the service more humbly. I try to really listen when I ask someone how they're doing. I help get the room ready for the service. I sit next to someone I don't know and ask about their lives. I am open and vulnerable for them. I am welcoming and kind. I thank the local director for her service.

I am present.

When it comes time to perform my song, I am ready for anything.

I have gotten out of the way.

## Salina

"Get dressed."

I have woken up at 12:30 a.m. It is Saturday night, fading into Sunday morning. I am living by myself for the first time, sleeping on a bare mattress on the floor of a nearly empty rental house.

I have just finished my sophomore year of engineering school. At a career fair I talked my way into a job, an internship. The head of engineering, the hiring manager, liked my hustle. Now I am living in Salina, Kansas, population fifty thousand, for the summer, working for a company that manufactures airport buses. It's not sexy, but it's an internship. I am learning a lot about what I don't want to do when I grow up.

I don't know anyone in town. I have no TV. That evening I called it early for a twenty-year-old and went to bed at 10:30 p.m. Now I am awake. The Voice has my attention.

"Get dressed."

It's July. Muggy. Still over eighty degrees in the middle of the night. I throw on some shorts and flip-flops and take a few deep breaths, trying to shake the remnants of sleep.

"Go for a walk."

"Wait, what? Oh, hell no!" My mind, my amygdala, is protesting. I don't know this town very well. Just cruising around the neighborhood past midnight doesn't seem like the safest strategy. My mind has more to say, more dangers to point out.

But I've heard the call.

I close my eyes and breathe deeply. I settle. I listen.

After a few breaths I know the destination. There is a park about half a mile away.

I look around my spartan house briefly, wondering if I will ever see it again. The deeper part of me is calm, composed, and tuned in. Nothing to fear. In the zone. Awake. This is not random. There is a reason. Now I just need to figure out what it is.

As I walk, the inner battle for my attention continues, my mind jumpy and pointing out all the dangers in the dark, the deeper part of me calm and focused, ignoring the mind's chatter.

Dialed in.

I reach the park in less than ten minutes. It doesn't take long to solve the mystery. I see a young man, about sixteen, sitting on a set of steps by the play structure, shoulders slumped. He has his back to me. As I approach, he startles a bit. Shoots me a nervous glance.

I give him one back.

Then I nod. "Hey."

"Oh. Hey." He's fiddling with something in his hands.

"Whatcha doin'?" He has been turned away from me, hands on his face. Now, he turns back to look at me. His eyes are red.

"Oh . . . I'm just sitting here trying to figure out why my life is so messed up." He pauses. I sense that he is harmless. I relax and wait.

"And . . . this." He shows me the knife in his hands. He shows me the marks on his wrists.

"Ahhh. I see." I sit down next to him on the steps. He has a table knife. He needs a Band-Aid, but he is in no immediate danger. His real wounds are so much deeper. Complicated. Severe. Life threatening. They are going to need more than a Band-Aid. We lock eyes for a long time. I'm calm, like my own internal storming ocean has settled to a mirror-surfaced lake.

"You don't wanna do that." I take a deep breath and hold out my hand. He looks at me. At my open hand. At my eyes. He gives me the knife and stares at his shoes.

"Yeah?" He says this blankly, lost in his pain.

I nod. "Yeah."

"I just . . ." His voice trails off. "Gaaahhhhhhh!" He started sobbing. I put my hand on his shoulder while he lets it all out.

"I know." I mutter this as much to myself as to him, my eyes tearing with his. We sit and talk for over an hour. I tell him my story. He exhales. He feels safe to share his. The details of our stories don't even matter. Pain is pain. We bond by the climbing structure, hidden in the dark.

He lets it all out. The frustration. The isolation. The loneliness. The stories. The heartbreak. The tears. All of it, out.

He starts to soften. He is lighter.

Eventually, he is ready to go home. I walk him back. He tells me that I have actually saved his life. I look away. I know he is being dramatic, that he wasn't going to kill himself with a table knife. He just needed a connection. He was hurting and didn't know how to help himself. He didn't know how to get help. How to communicate the complex mess of emotions and anxieties he was feeling.

He didn't know.

I am twenty. I stopped thinking about hurting myself four years earlier. I am in a good place. I am happy again. Confident. Life is good.

But still, the aftermath of my suffering is always with me, like a cloud. Maybe time heals all wounds. Maybe it hasn't been enough time. It doesn't take much to tap into my own darkness, to remember the isolation. As I told him my story in the playground, I realized I wasn't thinking about it as much anymore. I have some distance. I feel closer to being whole.

Here I am, finally emerging from my cloud. Finally able to stand strong.

And here is this kid in Salina. On the surface, he's nothing like me. If we were classmates, we probably wouldn't be friends. If I had seen him in the daylight, sitting on the steps, suffering, I wish I could tell you with confidence that for sure I'd go to him. That I'd listen carefully, with deep understanding and patience. I wish that were true.

The truth is, I'm sure I've walked past the same type of suffering nearly every day. Maybe I'm too busy. Maybe I'm stuck in my own head. Maybe I have judgments about the other person. Maybe I just don't know what to do. Maybe I'm scared. Maybe I'm somehow scared that their pain will be contagious, will reopen my own wounds, like how a drowning swimmer can take down a lifeguard if they're not careful. Maybe I'm not as strong as I'd like to think.

But on one hot summer night in Salina, I listen.

I still wonder if the whole summer job was just a setup for me to have this one conversation.

If it was, it was worth it.


## Mother's Shaker

A group of siblings has gathered at the family farmhouse. Their mother has just passed away. The hospital visits and the funeral are behind them. They can exhale. They have all come home; some drove, others had needed to fly. They are sitting around the kitchen table, just the four of them. It has been a long time since it was just the four of them. Their spouses and kids are in the other rooms, playing outside, or taking a quiet

"And this,

I do for love."

moment to sink inside themselves with their phones, ready to return to their lives.

The siblings are reliving their past, reliving the fights and the laughs that have happened in this house. The time a bit of spilled water turned into a raging food fight. The time the youngest daughter lost her first tooth eating corn. The time a bat somehow got into the house and their mother spent all afternoon chasing it around with a broom, shouting. It was the only time they had ever heard her swear. They laugh, the kind of laughter that mixes along with tears, the kind that lightens the heart.

They recall the amazing food their mother made. How they never ate out, every meal was at home—three meals a day from scratch. They marvel in comparison to their own modern lives.

They compare their favorite meals. Beef pot roast. Sloppy Joes. Green bean casserole. Jell-O salad. And pie. Always pie. Cherry from the tree in the backyard. Strawberry rhubarb. Raisin cream. The daughters have copied down all the recipes and they are excellent cooks as well. But somehow their creations are never quite the same as their mom's.

One remembers that before their mother would serve a meal, she had a special shaker. She would dust the last dish with it and then she was ready. "What was in the shaker?" asks the oldest brother. Puzzled looks and shaking heads. No one knows.

"It was shaped like an angel," says the youngest sister.

"Everything was shaped like an angel," says another. They all laugh and get lost in their memories for a bit. Another tear falls.

"Where is it?"

More shaking heads. No one knows. None of them have lived here for thirty years.

Some of mom's things have already been packed in boxes. The second daughter thinks she might know where the right box is. Cardboard and newspaper start piling up. It is a treasure hunt.

Four boxes in, they find the angel. She is yellow and light blue and faded. One of her wings is chipped. Mom had probably paid a quarter for her at a garage sale.

They gather closer; the secret is soon to be revealed. They lift the angel's head, anxious to find the source of mother's culinary genius.

The angel's insides are empty except for a tiny piece of paper. It is a note, blue pen in mother's cursive, that she had scribbled so long ago, perhaps in a quiet moment in between meals. Perhaps in a quiet moment of peace between the squabbles of her four kids. Perhaps after a prayer and a deep breath.

The short note summarizes mother's life.

"And this, I do for love."


## Shift

As a prisoner to our experience, life happens *to* us.

As we blossom and unfold, reaching for the sun, life happens *for* us.

As we gain our freedom and shake off the chains of our own making, and fly... life starts to happen *through* us.

Like a great starving beast
My body is quivering,
Fixed on the scent
Of Light

**HAFIZ**

# 17

# IN SERVICE
# TO LIFE

IT ALL comes down to this.

## Know Yourself

WHEN WE KNOW ourselves, we have a deep understanding of where inertia is taking us. We know
our own story, the highs and lows that have shaped
our lives. We understand the external systems that shape our
behavior—the expectations from our families, our community,
our social norms. We understand our own internal systems.
How our brains tend to focus on the negative to help keep us
safe. How our nervous systems create our level of stress or
relaxation.

When we know ourselves, we can be an observer to our
own experience. We can start to separate from the emotion
and drama that hold us in place. We can see the factors that
shape our lives, and make more conscious choices about what
we want. Awareness gives us choice. We have the map in our

hands. There's no need to wander. We can choose our own destination. We can choose who we want to be.

We find the map.

## Love Yourself

When we love ourselves, we let go of our emptiness. We acknowledge our True Self. We realize that we are so much more than this physical body we walk around in. We are creative sparks of energy. We can quiet our inner critic, designed to keep us safe, and instead practice self-compassion. We can slow down, settle, and tune in. We learn to be grateful for every moment, every breath, realizing each moment as a miracle. Our love for all of life lights up our inner spark, removing the shackles on our True Self and unleashing a wave of creativity. This creativity is the fuel that moves us toward our new destination.

We recognize our true nature.

## Master Yourself

Ah, here is the hard part. When we see the map of our lives clearly and realize that we are responsible for our own lives, there can be no one else to blame. When we take responsibility for our own development, we mature. We move away from stagnation. We move from "life happens *to* us" to "life happens *for* us." We are responsible for every aspect of how we respond to life. We shift to optimism, and with that shift the aperture of our lives widens toward freedom. We are conscious of our choices. We manifest our own futures. We see every moment, even the challenging ones, *especially* the challenging ones, as an opportunity for growth. We even learn to have gratitude for those challenges. We are never victims again. We learn to tune in to our inner guidance. We are brave enough, secure in our own experience, to remove our filters and meet life fully. We know who we are. Where we are going. We are determined to get there. We feel it in our bodies in a way that is full and true and right. We feel every atom in alignment with our internal compass. We feel The Full Body Yes.

We take responsibility and action.

## Compassion in Action

When we are full and whole, we are filled with joy. We are filled with life. We feel compelled to give back to life, to serve. When we serve others, we move away from loneliness. We become aware of others. We realize that their experiences are not so different from our own. We become aware of their needs. Just as we recognize our own shining True Self, we begin to see this True Self in others.

We move away from feeling separate from others. We see how we are part of a larger whole that cannot be broken into disconnected parts of "us" and "them."

We remove the internal barriers that have kept us from our True Self. We remove the barriers we've built to keep others and their True Self away from us. We are inseparable from the rest of life. We see and love others as if they are an extension of our own being.

We evolve from "life happens *for* us" to "life happens *through* us."

We take action. We serve others. We serve all of life.

Our love of all life shines brightly and is reflected, amplified by those around us.

Our bodies, minds, and emotions settle into a deep congruency, every atom aligned. We feel joy, unbounded goodness. We *become* joy.

We *become* The Full Body Yes.

Free.

The sky where we live

Is no place to lose

Your wings

So love, love, love

**HAFIZ**

# 18

# THE UNIVERSE
# SENT ME JOY

WE ARE IN downtown Santa Barbara. I am shopping with my family. The air is crisp—the kind of California cool where you need a jacket when the sun's not shining directly on you.

I don't feel like shopping. I walk aimlessly, no interest in the fall sales. No interest in boba tea, pastries, or the scent of pizza slices wafting from the wood fire. My mind is too full. Too heavy with questions. I am going through something. It's ugly. I feel like I am being torn apart from the inside.

I let them go ahead while I wander.

There is no one I can call to share this problem. No hotline where I can take a number and get assistance. I know I have to figure it out myself. The weight of that thought is crushing. I fall deep inside myself, into a giant underground cavern with no entrance. I can only hope for an exit.

I need to sit down. I can no longer walk and think at the same time. I amble for blocks, half in my body, searching for a place to sit. Searching for anything that might tame the pain. Searching for truth.

I give up. I need help. I have questions for the Universe. I have been asking for days. I sense the answers are all right there, but I can't hear. I'm not receiving. It's like I am playing an old-timey radio and I am tuned in to the wrong station. I keep messing with the dial and getting static.

I mutter out loud. "I don't know. I need some help here."

I notice a tiny bench. It is a two-person bench, with an armrest between the two seats. Intimate. There is already some-one sitting in one half. From a distance I think it might be a thirteen-year-old boy. I decide he won't mind if I sit next to him. I have a seat and close my eyes, feeling the sunshine on my face. I let out a long exhale.

"Hi! What's your name?" I hear a bright voice beside me. I am nudged from my thought coma. I blink and look for the voice.

"Oh, hi. I'm Scott. What's your name?" I say on autopilot. The voice is coming from the person in the other seat, who turns out to be a young woman. Maybe twenty years old, Black, with short, cropped hair. Androgynous. She has a big smile.

"I'm Joy." Her eyes are clear, very clear. I let out a short laugh.

"Of *course* you are," I say, smiling. Joy doesn't respond. She just smiles back.

"Wow. That was fast," I think to myself.

I am on full alert. I look at her with deep curiosity. She looks back with no filter. Just those clear, clear eyes.

"What are you up to, Joy?"

"I'm traveling. I'm on a journey. My mission is to help people find their spark. To help them light it up." She speaks with no hesitation. No shield.

I smile. After a long pause, I say, "That's interesting. That's my mission too." She smiles back as if she had known that all along. We sit for a bit, taking each other in.

I take a long, deep breath and exhale slowly. I turn my body to face her. I nod and shake my head as if summoning the courage to cliff jump. "Okay, Joy, I've got one for you."

She nods at me to continue, and I ask her the question I have for the Universe. She doesn't flinch. She tilts her head and considers it. Then she starts talking. She has the answer I have been looking for. The one I need in this moment. The one that calms the storm inside. That allows me to settle.

In turn, I have some answers that she has been searching for. That she needs to hear. That allows something inside her to settle.

After we share our stories, our truths, we make more small talk out of habit. But now words seem obsolete, like a wool scarf on a summer day. We let them go. We become still. We smile. We allow ourselves to just be.

My inner tension has evaporated. The churning seas inside my stomach are now a glassy pool, ready to reflect the infinite sky. I feel a sense of deep contentment. I just want to close my eyes and marinate in the feeling.

We sit quietly in the sun for a long, long while, taking it all in.

In my time of need, in my darkness, when I couldn't hear it any other way, the Universe has sent me Joy.

## Headed to Baseball

"Ugh! I should be back at the office. I have work to do!"

I'm stuck in traffic. There's been an incident on the 101. I left at 3:15 p.m. so I could get to my son's little league baseball game in time to get the field ready for our game today. I've been coaching the team for the past couple of years.

Today, I'm annoyed. My schedule is completely stacked. There's a customer issue that's bubbling up and will likely require my attention. The work has piled up on my desk and feels like a monster, ready to devour me on my return. There are people on my team who wanted time from me today. I had to say no. And, I'm leaving in the middle of the day. Even though we have flex time, leaving before 5 p.m. just feels wrong. Makes me feel guilty. I was already feeling stressed about the whole situation. Now this traffic slowdown is piling on, adding another brick to my wall of irritation.

My inner talk track has gone dark.

"Seriously, what am I doing?" I have work and I'm leaving at three to go coach baseball? I never should have agreed to manage the team. Why can't someone else help me get the field ready?

"Gaaaaaaah!" I let out a frustrated growl as the traffic slows. We are moving from three lanes to two. There are two cars in the far-right lane that have gotten into a scuffle. The drivers are discussing things on the shoulder.

"People need to learn to drive. Come on!" I say out loud. My funk continues. I resume my inner list of complaints about life.

As I inch past the accident, I catch a look at the face of the man driving the car that was the back half of the fender-bender. He looks spent. In that moment I realize that he is an actual person as well. He isn't just an actor in my play—there to irritate and slow me down. He is like me, just trying to get by. Maybe he is also stupid-busy. Maybe he has been rushing to pick up his daughter from school. Maybe he is late on his bills and wondering if he is going to keep putting up with his boss to keep the checks flowing. Maybe he had glanced down at his buzzing phone one too many times and missed seeing the brake lights in front of him. Maybe he is feeling self-loathing as he has to find his registration and insurance docs from the glovebox. After this latest disaster, maybe his wife will finally follow through on the divorce she has been threatening him with.

Seeing his face shifts something for me, wakes me from my bad dream. I shake my head, take a deep breath, and reconsider. What else is true?

I'm focused on what's wrong. But what's right? What else is true?

Actually, I have a long list.

First, I love my son. I enjoy watching him play baseball. I enjoy seeing him learn and grow. I enjoy watching him practice and get better every day. I enjoy playing catch with him in the front yard.

I love baseball. It was my favorite sport as a kid. Coaching allows me to be ten years old again, to be out on the field in spring with the smell of the freshly cut outfield.

I love coaching, coming up with new drills, new combinations of lineups. I love hanging out with the guys, seeing their joy as they're released from school and unleashed onto the grass. I share their sense of freedom.

I'm incredibly grateful that I have a job where I can leave at 3 p.m. on a Tuesday to do what I need to do. I realize many people aren't as fortunate.

My list continues.

I am *choosing* to be here.

One more powerful memory hits me. When I was a kid, I absolutely treasured the times my dad would play catch with me. Often, he was too busy. I had a pitch-back, a springy net that I would throw the ball to and it would return it. I spent hours in front of that thing, practicing my craft, waiting until it got dark, hoping my dad would have enough energy to throw for a while after working in the field all day. The pitch-back was functional but a poor substitute for time with my dad.

During those long sessions alone, a thought was starting to form. If I ever had a son, if he ever asked me to play catch, no matter how tired or busy I was, I would always say yes.

In the car, I smile at the memory. I have come full circle. I'm not frustrated with my dad. I understand him. I have compassion for him. I am him.

*I play two scenarios forward.*

In the first one, I spent thirty-five minutes in the car complaining to myself about how life is getting in my way. About all the things I *have* to do. When I show up at the field I storm around, getting things ready for the boys. When the lawnmower won't start, I throw my body around and curse like a sailor. I can't figure it out. I pound the top of the mower with my hand. Curse some more. I give up and decide the dirt infield doesn't need to be raked anyway.

As the other coaches from our team arrive, I testily share that I've already been there for a half an hour by myself. They become quiet, withdrawn around me. They have also left work early. Have their own problems. Have the same tearing guilt as they're stretched between their work and home lives.

As the other team's coach arrives, he asks why the field hasn't been raked. I complain about the mower. He huffs off. Says he'll do it himself. A few minutes later I wince as I hear the mower cough to life. I watch the other coach prepare the field. I stand by, feeling impotent. That was my job. As the boys arrive, I have no patience. I'm short with them. I expect full compliance to my commands. They all annoy me.

Our pre-game drills are crisp. I'm shouting at the boys. I sense a bit of fear in them as they move from one drill to another. I notice that Seth has stayed behind in the dugout. From the third baseline I shout, "Get out here!" He does not get out here. After a couple of attempts I storm to the dugout.

"Dude, what the hell? Let's go!"

Seth tears up. By the time I soften and try to talk to him, it's too late. He can't hear me. He goes to sit next to his mom on the bleachers. She tries to encourage him back to the game. It's not happening. After ten minutes she finally relents. He's a mess. She's nearly carrying him to the car. She mouths "I'm sorry" to me and they go home. I can see the disappointment and guilt in her eyes. Seth misses the next three weeks of baseball.

It's quiet in the dugout. We force a few testosterone-filled shouts of encouragement during the game. There are temper tantrums and petty arguments. There are grim smiles and tight jaws. When it's over we pack up quickly in silence and go home.

In the second scenario, I spend thirty-five minutes in the car recounting all the things I'm grateful for. How life is providing me opportunity to grow every day. To learn a little bit more about myself and others. A little bit more about love. I remember how much I love baseball. How much I love my son. How much I love hanging out with the guys. How much I enjoy being with the other dads.

I show up with gratitude that I'm able to serve my community in this way. The mower won't start, but after a few deep breaths I remember that you have to wiggle the choke and then turn the key just past halfway until it fires. Once it starts, it runs like a boss. As I drag the dirt infield, I enjoy the patterns the iron mesh rake makes. It reminds me of tractor work on the farm.

As the other coaches on our team arrive, I ask how their day has been. I can see the busy on their faces. I thank them for their service. I share my appreciation for how they left their own jobs early. I think of something specific each one has done to help, and share my gratitude for that. I ask them what their favorite memory of playing baseball was when they were kids. I listen patiently, smiling. I ask them what they think their son's favorite memory will be from this season. I share something positive about each of their sons that I've observed. I can see them soften. I can see them arriving. I can see their shift from busy to present happen ever so slowly, like the mower coming to life. Once they're present and get going, they run like a boss.

When the other team's coach arrives, we trade some friendly banter. He thanks me for having the field ready. I find exactly the right mix of competitive teasing and warmth. He's laughing as he heads to his team's dugout. I hear him shouting happy encouragement to his boys. He's crackling with energy.

When the kids all arrive, we head to the grass in center field. We have a funny song that we've made up together to cheer before we get started. I laugh with them. I have the patience to channel their freedom, their energy, into our craft, finding the delicate balance between the organization of a team, and the loose freedom of each individual.

I am aware when Seth is quiet and not paying attention. While the boys take the field, I ask one of the other dads to manage the game for a bit. I go to Seth. I kneel on the ground in front of him, search his eyes, listen. He tells me his story. I share a few caring words of encouragement. We have a real conversation. I see him. After a few minutes, he moves from his head to his body. He nods. He's ready to go. He thrives. At the end of the season his mom tells me through tears that baseball has been the only good thing in Seth's life. She thanks me for being there for him.

The boys are loud. They are cracking jokes. They bounce from the dugout to the field. They bat with great enthusiasm. They cheer each other on from a place of pure joy.

When it's over, they ask when our next game is, eager for another chance to feel this way.

I *wish* I could tell you that at each juncture like this one in my life, I chose option two.

Compassion is so simple.

Compassion can be so hard.

The Full Body Yes can be elusive. Yet...

It's as near as our heartbeat.

As close as our breath.

Always right there for us to step into.

And I

(sigh)

I am a work in progress.

# NOTES

1   *Encyclopedia Britannica*, s.v., "Theileriasis," britannica.com/science/theileriasis.

2   Kristin Neff, *Self-Compassion: The Proven Power of Being Kind to Yourself* (William Morrow, 2011).

3   Robert A. Emmons and Michael E. McCullough, "Counting Blessings Versus Burdens: An Experimental Investigation of Gratitude and Subjective Well-Being in Daily Life," *Journal of Personality and Social Psychology* 84, no. 2 (2003), doi.org/10.1037//0022-3514.84.2.377.

4   Robert A. Emmons, *Thanks!: How the New Science of Gratitude Can Make You Happier* (Houghton Mifflin, 2007).

5   James Clear, *Atomic Habits: An Easy & Proven Way to Build Good Habits & Break Bad Ones* (Avery, 2018).

6   Alison Wood Brooks, "Get Excited: Reappraising Pre-Performance Anxiety as Excitement," *Journal of Experimental Psychology* 143, no. 3 (2014), doi.org/10.1037/a0035325.

7   Viktor Frankl, *Man's Search for Meaning* (Beacon Press, 2006). Frankl first published this work in 1946.

8   Philip Brickman and Dan Coates, "Lottery Winners and Accident Victims: Is Happiness Relative?" *Journal of Personality and Social Psychology* 36, no. 8 (1978), doi.org/10.1037/0022-3514.36.8.917.

9   John M. Darley and Daniel Batson, "'From Jerusalem to Jericho': A Study of Situational and Dispositional Variables in Helping Behavior," *Journal of Personality and Social Psychology* 27, no. 1 (1973), doi.org/10.1037/h0034449.

10  PBS, *The Brain with David Eagleman*, episode 5, "Why Do I Need You?" aired November 11, 2015, 55:11.

# ACKNOWLEDGMENTS

LIFE IS A team sport. I am nothing without the people who have shaped me.

It starts with family, and I am blessed to be rich with family.

A deepest thank you to my wife, Aparna. I knew immediately. She is as strong, smart, and selfless as anyone I've ever known. I am a better person because of you. I'm grateful for your support, your care, and your love.

To my amazing kids—Kameron and Anjali. It is a blessing and a joy to be your father. I learn something new from you nearly every day. You are my sunshine.

Thank you to my parents, Ed and Jeri. My mom instilled in me a belief that I could achieve anything I put my mind to. My dad shared that most of the world's problems (especially my own) could be solved with a good attitude. They showed me how to live.

To Steve, Tom, Julie, and Karla—thank you for setting the bar high. Thank you for your love and light.

One evening Soren Gordhamer and I were driving back together from an event. Soren scrunched his eyebrows, tilted his head toward me, and, without hesitation or filter, said, "The

Universe told me to tell you that it's time to write your book."
This is how our relationship works. Soren, who leads the Wisdom 2.0 conference series, has given me and so many others a place to share our voice, to express a greater sense of our being. Without him the world would be a smaller place.

He was right. It was time. Thank you, Soren.

I feel incredibly privileged to work at LinkedIn, where compassion is embedded in everything we do. Our longtime CEO, Jeff Weiner, would openly talk about his own meditation practice. He regularly speaks about compassion. He puts it into practice and leads by example. Without Jeff and the umbrella of safety he created around these topics, I wouldn't be able to do this work.

Thank you to Ryan Roslansky, LinkedIn's current CEO. I was reporting to Ryan for a couple of years when I led customer operations. I was volunteering as our exec sponsor for our mindfulness programs. Ryan kept challenging me to go further, to think bigger. With Ryan's encouragement and support, we created the role of head of mindfulness and compassion programs, one of the first of its kind in the business world.

Thanks to Shannon McNally. Together, along with our volunteer community, we've built something truly amazing at LinkedIn. Thank you to Kevin Delaney, for the space and encouragement to do this work.

To my wise friends and colleagues David Bruner, Lori Schwanbeck, Shauna Shapiro, Sarah Dowling, Brad Foy, Dick Wallace, and Tom Walsh. I appreciate your stories and wisdom, some of which I have humbly included here.

To Bernard Poirier and Yit Louie, who joined me without fail as we built a practice together week by week. Your partnership gave life to the work and increased the joy along the way.

Back when my first draft was just forming, a few brave souls jumped in and agreed to provide feedback. Some were friends

I'd known for a long time and I knew that some of these stories would surprise them. Some were new friends and I knew a few of these stories would surprise them. They were thoughtful, kind, and honest, and helped me shape the way I thought about the content, and my life, in a meaningful way. I am very grateful. Thank you Mick Lunzer, Chad Brown, Dave Hew, Sudha Ranganathan, Alec Kassin, Abbie Layton, Annie Dow, and Lisa Boston, and to everyone else who provided encouragement along the way.

As a first-time author, I was so happy to have Lisa Thomas-Tench as my editor. I knew I needed a partner, and she was exactly what I needed. She helped shape and form these stories into a cohesive narrative. Her encouragement and genius helped me stay focused and made me a better writer. I'm grateful for the wisdom and sharp eye of my other editors, Melissa Edwards and Amanda Lewis. Their expertise in the nuances of this work is invaluable.

Finally, thank you to my teacher and guide, Harold Klemp. Your guidance is always appreciated. I know you and your teachings will always be with me.

# ABOUT THE AUTHOR

SCOTT SHUTE has journeyed from America's heartland across the world, discovering more about what tears people apart and what brings them together. As vice president of global customer operations at LinkedIn, he led an international team of one thousand customer service employees supporting over seven hundred million network members around the world. Today, as head of mindfulness and compassion, he is implementing his vision of changing work from the inside out by building industry-leading mindfulness programs and operationalizing compassion.

# MISSION: CHANGE WORK (AND THE WORLD) FROM THE INSIDE OUT

HI FRIENDS,

Thanks for spending time with me. If you've gotten this far, then maybe you've found we share some common values and goals. Maybe you're interested in taking the next step in our relationship. My mission is to change work (and the world) from the inside out. I'd love to be of service to you, if you'd like that, in your own organization, or your own life.

Here are a few ways we might work together.

**Copies for your organization:** Want to buy copies of this book for your organization? Contact me about bulk discounts and special offers at thefullbodyyes.com.

**Speaking for your event:** Fireside chats, keynotes, Zoom gatherings. Whatever the event, I promise to make it engaging, fun, powerful, and memorable.

**Retreats and workshops:** Let's go deeper. This work can be incredibly powerful when we give it the energy of time and attention. Spending a weekend or an afternoon together might just be life-changing.

**Coaching:** I work with a select few executives and individuals who are committed to joining me in changing work from the inside out.

**Video training:** Can't get to a workshop or retreat, but want to go deeper? A master class video series might be just for you.

**Photography:** I'm inspired by the wild and beautiful places in the world. I try to capture this wonder and my sense of awe with photography. You can find my best work at scottshute photos.com. If you're interested in ordering something beautiful for your home—first of all, thank you!—and second, know that almost all of the proceeds I get from photography go to charity.

You can find out more about these and other offerings at scottshute.com.

## A Favor—Will You Help Me Change Work (and the World) from the Inside Out?

Real talk for a second. I could use your help.

Modern books are judged by the universal recognition of an Amazon review. If this is something you're up for, please write a review. I would really appreciate it, and it's meaningful for the book's success.

## Let's Start the Conversation

Don't be a stranger. Send me an email or reach out via LinkedIn to discuss one or more options for your team and your organization. Or just let me know if you liked the book, or maybe which story was your favorite.

I'm looking forward to hearing from you.

info@scottshute.com
scottshute.com
in scottshute
@scottshutephotos
@scottshute1